GREG NORMAN

GREG NORMAN

IRONBARK LEGENDS

IRONBARK
Pan Macmillan Australia

First published 1999 in Ironbark by Pan Macmillan Australia Pty Limited
St Martins Tower, 31 Market Street, Sydney

National Library of Australia
cataloguing-in-publication data:

Greg Norman : Ironbark legends

ISBN 0 330 361767.

1. Norman, Greg, 1955- . 2. Golfers - Australia - Anecdotes.
3. Golfers - Australia - Biography. (Series : Ironbark legends).

796.352092

Designed by Mark Thacker, Big Cat Design
Printed in Australia by Australian Book Connection

Photo acknowledgements: pp. xi, 1, 8, 11, 18, 25, 26, 27 (bottom), 31, 32, 35, 37, 39, 40, 42, 43, 50, 52, 55, 56, 57, 60 (bottom), 63, 65, 67, 69, 71, 76, 77, 79, 83, 85, 86-87 (top right), 88 (top), 93, 102, 103, 105, 111 (bottom), 112, 113, Allsport Australia; pp. 3, 21, 41, 49, 75, Sportsphoto Agency; pp. 10, 47, 53, 62, 91, 92, Bernie McGuire; p. 27 (top), 97, 98, Varley Picture Agency; p. 58, Sergio Dionisio; pp. 59, 61 Chicot Agency; p. 60 (top), Juergen Hasenkopf; p. 78, Jim Moriarty; p. 80, Bob Scott; p. 81, Australian Picture Library; p. 101, Wagner Photography; p. 107, Mark Lee.

Every endeavour has been made to source the photographs and to contact copyright holders to obtain the necessary permission for use of photographs and other material in this book. Any person who may have been inadvertently overlooked should contact the publisher.

CONTENTS

A GOLFER OF DESTINY

His constant companion, fate steps every inch of the way with Greg Norman as he treks the fairways of championship golf. Norman is acutely aware of the presence, resigning himself without complaint to harsh mishaps dealt out, grateful for any good fortunes bestowed. Norman, sport's internationally famous Great White Shark, is a golfer of destiny.

Golf has produced perhaps a handful of more accomplished master competitors, more successful certainly if the record book is to be the judge, but none more charismatic. None with Norman's magnetic flair, dynamism and sense of drama. He is a gallery favourite, simply because he is teeing it up out there and making it happen. Make something happen. Excitement engulfs him and you feel you want to be part of it.

In Australia, a nation that continues to produce an astonishing diversity of sports stars, Greg Norman is a golfing legend. Hence this tribute and the coterie of distinguished contributors who have enthusiastically crafted the stories that follow. These personal accounts and anecdotes are written from different angles and, when pieced together, provide a captivating picture of a unique Australian.

PHIL TRESIDDER

GEORGE BUSH

May 12, 1999

Greg Norman is a true legend to the game of golf.
I am proud to consider him a friend.

He has shown all golf fans an awful lot of class,
both in victory and in defeat.

They broke the mould when they made this
golfing legend.

*George Bush was President of the United States from the years
1989 to 1993 and remains one of golf's greatest and most popular patrons.

THE GUTS AND THE GAME

by Charlie Earp

A number of people have played a role in the astonishing rise of Greg Norman to sporting fame, but in the early days, when the young Shark's future hung in the balance, it was Charlie Earp who took him under his wing at Royal Queensland and sent him out as a free spirit to achieve some of golf's greatest conquests. They remain the staunchest of friends today.

4

Greg Norman was unannounced and virtually unnoticed when he joined Royal Queensland Golf Club in 1974, but I was aware that the blond kid with bundles of enthusiasm had plenty of talent.

He had lit up the amateur section of the Australian Open the previous year at Royal Queensland with a couple of fine rounds, and had done it with style. Greg had played most of his early golf at Virginia, about 10 minutes' drive from the club, and had a real look of success about him. Virginia has produced a lot of good players, notably Wayne Grady, but Greg switched clubs because his mother, Toini, joined Royal Queensland at the same time and we had pretty good practice facilities.

The Normans had barely come through the gate and their names were on the honour boards in the clubhouse. During their initial year at the club, Toini won the associates championship and Greg notched the junior and senior club championships.

Page 3: The year is 1985—and this is the profile of a winner. Greg Norman led the Australian team to victory in the Dunhill Nations Cup at St. Andrews.
Opposite: The young Shark's broad smile mirrors his joy as tournament victories tumbled into his lap in 1986, including the British Open at Turnberry. ABC commentator Norman May salutes Greg Norman, voted by sports editors across the country as Australia's 1986 Sportsman of the Year.
Below left: Caught deep in thought. Norman's first coach, Charlie Earp, contemplates the Shark's exciting future.

Greg and I gradually became closer, and spent time together on the practice range. As long as I've known him Greg has been a good listener and unfailingly polite. He was an outgoing kid, but never pushy. It might be difficult to believe of Greg Norman but, in those days, I reckon he had an inferiority complex which made him try extra hard to be outgoing, happy and helpful. Even then it was evident that he was very single-minded: he knew what he wanted and ensured every bit of talent was utilised. Greg never wasted anything.

Towards the end of 1974 Greg made a decision to turn pro, but some people were telling him that he wouldn't do any good in Brisbane and that he'd have to go to Sydney to be successful. I knew that wasn't the case, but he decided to go south to start an apprenticeship with Billy McWilliam, a mate of mine at Beverley Park Golf Club. Billy had nurtured the early careers of Bruce Crampton and Bruce Devlin and had apparently been given an assurance by the New South Wales PGA that Greg would be released to play tournaments on invitation.

Below: Unruly blond hair and sponsorship logos missing, the rookie pro lashes into a fairway shot at the 1983 New South Wales Open at Concord Golf Club, Sydney, with an admiring audience in the backgound.

But things didn't work out. After three or four months Greg wanted to return to Brisbane for a number of reasons. He wasn't getting the time he wanted for practice and was working nights at a driving range. He became frustrated with the situation. He's also a homely sort of guy and I'm certain he missed his family and the close friends he'd made during his amateur days in Brisbane.

Greg phoned me and asked if there was any chance of completing his apprenticeship with me at the Royal Queensland pro shop. I couldn't see any problem and Greg promptly jumped into his Ford Cortina and drove the 800 kilometres from Sydney to discuss the matter further.

He arrived at our house mid-morning and sat in the lounge room with my wife, Margaret, and me where we confirmed the arrangement. Marg and I knew there wouldn't be any problem because we were aware that Greg was a good type of lad and very motivated.

He shook my hand and immediately drove back to Sydney to pack his gear and finalise his affairs. That showed how tough the kid was: he drove from Sydney, then had no hesitation in turning around to head back without any sleep.

Greg started on $38 a week and worked with my other trainee at the time, Jim Barden. We always worked two shifts in the shop—7 a.m. to 3 p.m. and 10 a.m. to 6 p.m.—which meant the boys had ample time to practice and play.

Greg was a willing worker and never whinged about anything. About the only aversion he had was picking up balls on the practice range. Greg was fascinated and very enthusiastic about golf clubs. Indeed, he would spend lots of time tinkering and fiddling around with different clubs.

Above: The US Open of 1984 up for grabs at Winged Foot. Coach Charlie Earp (pictured) flew to New York to take over the caddie job. Norman was to tie Fuzzy Zoeller at the final hole, only to lose the next day in a play-off.

7

And he was always interested in the golf swing, referring constantly to a pile of books and magazines in the back of the pro shop. Greg modelled his game on Jack Nicklaus and was always a stronger hitter of the ball than the other young guys.

We'd always discuss issues of the day in the shop—sport, politics and life in general. That's part of the process. I wanted it to be an environment where the trainees also learnt to converse and present themselves.

I have no doubt that Greg's interaction with the members at Royal Queensland had a lasting influence on his career. When he and Jim Barden first received invitations to play tournaments in other states, a few of the members threw in money to help with their expenses. He learnt to mix easily with everyone in those days.

And he enjoyed playing for money. That hardened him up a bit and I reckon he took a few decent cheques from the members when he was a trainee!

Greg beat Gerry Taylor in a play-off to win the Queensland trainees championship in 1975, then defended it in 1976 to win by 16 strokes. He was going very well in pro-ams but his first big tournament as a professional was the 1976 Queensland Open at Keperra where he finished third behind John Dyer.

By then Greg was ready for bigger things. At that stage he was hitting the ball very high like the Americans and I suggested that he needed to learn to keep the ball low with 'punch' or 'squeeze' shots if he was to be successful in Europe. Greg was a bit sceptical. He was a guy who wanted you to prove things to him before he took it as gospel.

I told him he'd pay the penalty in Europe if he didn't learn. I spun him a yarn that his tee shots in Scotland would finish in Paris if he didn't adapt his game to control the ball in the wind.

Around this time Tom McNaughton, a Scottish pro who had played quite a few British Opens before moving to Queensland, was practising at Royal Queensland and I called him over to talk to Greg. Tom told him it was necessary to keep the ball 'as high as the quail flies' when playing in Europe.

So Greg started work on perfecting the punch shot. Within a couple of days he was hitting them beautifully.

That adaptability has been one of the keys to his great success. Consider all the great golfers of this century and there are probably no more than 50 who were real champions, capable of winning anywhere in the world. That's the true test of a great player— someone who can play in America one week, Australia the next, South Africa and then go to Europe and be competitive everywhere.

Golfers like Sarazen, Snead, Locke, Hagen, Jones, Hogan, Palmer, Nicklaus, Player, Thomson, von Nida, Ballesteros, Nick Price, Norman ... there are not a lot of them.

When Greg won the West Lakes Classic late in 1976 he was

Opposite: The ball flies high in a cloud of sand as Greg Norman escapes from a bunker in the 1988 US Masters at Augusta National.

ready to take on the world. Then, when he was successful in the Martini International in Britain the next year we knew he really had something special.

It was significant that James Marshall was involved as his first manager. I don't know what Greg's feelings towards James are these days but, from where I sit, he had a hell of an impact on his career.

Marshall was a tough Englishman who taught Greg a lot about business and about not being a sucker. He opened sponsorship opportunities and was strict with the type of advertising deals he allowed Greg to become involved with. At that stage in Greg's career I thought Marshall played an important role.

I can remember the day Greg left Brisbane on his first overseas trip. He was 21 and had received an invitation to play in Japan after winning the West Lakes Classic.

His mother and I were at the airport and I don't mind admitting I had tears in my eyes. I thought, 'This kid has the guts to do it on his own. He has the guts and the game to really give it a shake anywhere he wants.'

Right: The Stars and Stripes flies above the Winged Foot clubhouse, and it's a packed gallery around the first tee as Greg Norman fires his first blow in the 1984 US Open. He lost in a play-off, but his American tour career was truly up and away.
Opposite: The Shark anxiously watches the flight of this drive in the 1997 Desert Classic at Emirates, Dubai.

...adaptability has been one of the keys to his great success. Consider all the great golfers of this century and there are probably no more than 50 who were real champions, capable of winning anywhere in the world.

SUCH IS THE MAGIC AND JOY OF A FATHER–SON RELATIONSHIP

Merv Norman

Greg Norman's father talks of the profound relationship between father and son. Norman Snr, a highly successful engineer, recognised early on that young Greg would be a high achiever and could stand out from the mob. A father's intuition was spot on, not necessarily in golf, yet golf was to emerge the big winner.

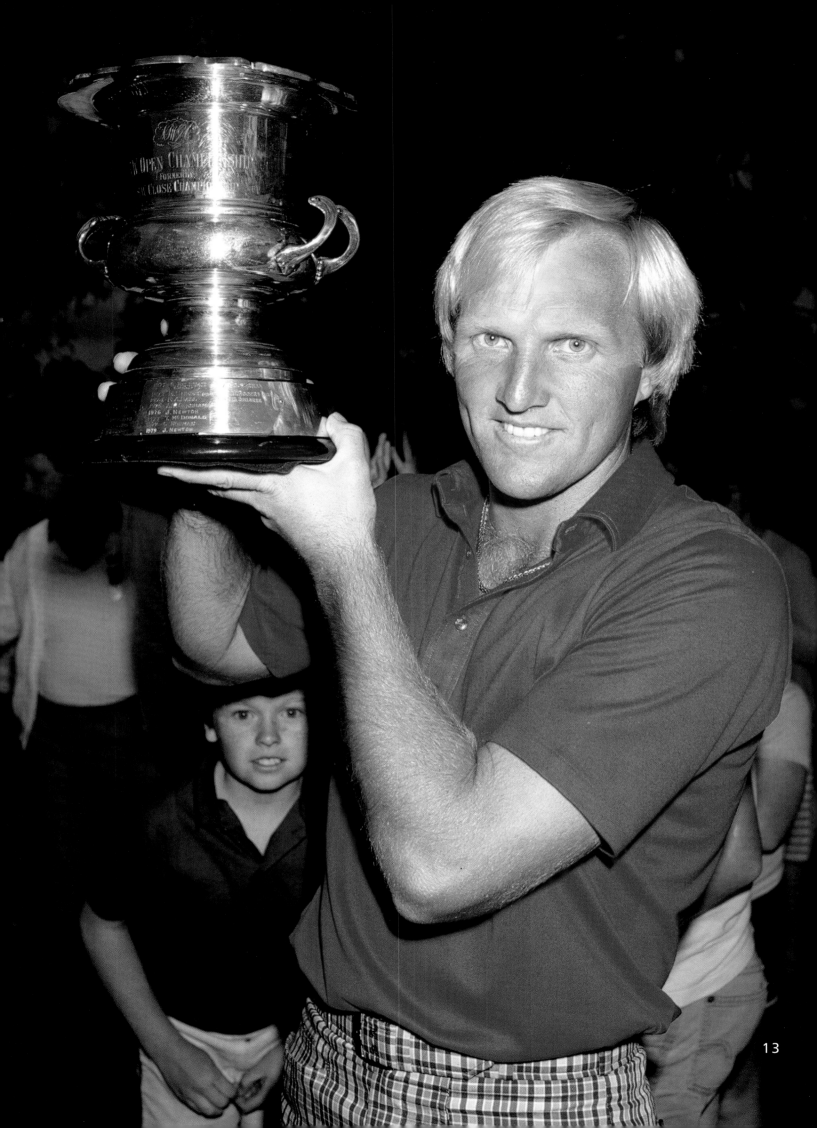

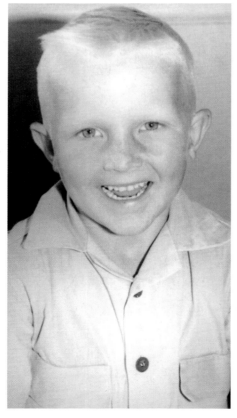

One of the outstanding and wonderful facets of a father and son relationship is that each sees the other differently from the way they see any other male. Each also expects more of the other than they expect of any other person.

Attitude to life, dignity, integrity, morality, the ability to achieve and achievements, self- and mutual respect, and fatherly love, are just a minuscule sample of the often unspoken yet prevalent desirable components of living that occur, or, I believe, should occur in the relationship from its beginning. When it exists the relationship is forever, and it is special and unique.

I have had the fortune to experience such a relationship with my father, and with Greg, and to observe it occurring between Greg and his son. They are the relationships which encompass the actions and reactions of a nuturing society.

The relationship between a mother and son, a mother and daughter, and between siblings is certainly no less loving and supportive—but it is different.

Page 13: Another shining trophy is paraded as Greg Norman's victory campaign gains momentum.

Opposite, top: A young Greg in 1963, pictured with his family—mother Toini, sister Janis, and father Merv.

Opposite, bottom: Early pictures of Greg, growing up in Rowes Bay, Townsville, Queensland.

This page, above right: His parents' favourite photo—the young fisherman in January 1969, age 13, proudly showing off his catch, a coral trout. Greg and the ocean have been enduring companions.

This page, bottom: The snowy-haired young Greg and his schoolmates departing from Townsville by plane for a Queensland schoolboy rugby league competition in Brisbane, 1966.

15

This page: Young Greg has that Tom Sawyer look, very much the outdoor adventurer with his mates (top and middle left). He's seen in Aspley High School uniform in 1970 (middle right) and in 1971, at age 16, on the course at Virginia Golf Club (right) for an early round with his father.

Opposite: Serious business as Greg and his schoolmates, supervised by an official, weigh in for the 1966 Queensland Under-six-stone rugby league championship. Good judges predicted a bright football career ahead for Greg, but golf was to become his passion.

From the time that most fathers first hold our sons in our arms we have an innate drive to inculcate them with behavioural patterns and knowledge in all its forms. The manner in which we do this, and the responses we receive, are as varied as the range of personalities that exist among human beings.

My father's 'teachings' remain with me. Amongst them was: 'If you undertake a task, do it well and to the best of your ability.'

It would be ridiculous and untruthful to suggest that there are never barriers to the interchange of thoughts or statements between a father and son. On the contrary, these barriers are numerous and may encounter a rough passage in the transfer process, but they are never impermeable. Mutual learning and understanding prevails, although it is neither acknowledged nor denied at the time, or perhaps at any time in the future.

From my experience, it is indisputable that the period of time between the presentation and acceptance of exchanged philosophies is lessened with the passage of time. Such is the magic and joy of a father–son relationship.

When Greg was about ten years of age, I had formed an unspoken opinion that he possessed certain attributes that would

Below: Parents Merv and Toini ready for a round. No question where Greg discovered his love of golf. Toini has been an avid golfer since the age of 21, and has won the associates championship at Royal Queensland Golf Club eight times.

permit him to become a high achiever and stand out from the mob. In physical activities he would attempt, with vigour, any challenge that was placed before him. He would pursue these activities until he became competent at them. He also displayed consideration for those around him.

At that stage, and for some years, none of these pursuits was paramount and academic subjects were an anathema to him, the latter of some discomfort to me.

I have strong recollections from our children's school years of encouraging them to think when presented with a problem and to try to resolve the problem within the bounds of what they had been taught and what they had, supposedly, learned at that stage, rather than present the problem to me, or to someone else, for a quick-fix answer without the necessity for them to apply their own mental abilities.

There were times when this attitude of mine provoked dead silence from the study tables in their bedrooms. I was quite firm but not incorrigible in this matter; an attitude which, while not easy for them or me, provided a platform that, I have observed, has placed Greg in good stead, particularly in the development of his golfing career and business activities.

I had to wait some years before my deliberately unspoken opinion was vindicated.

Last year, 1998, when my wife, Toini, and I were on a United

Above: A long blond mane made Greg a prominent figure on the fairways. Here, in 1980, he is posing for a shot at Royal Queensland Golf Club.

States visit to see Greg, Laura, and their children, Morgan-Leigh and Gregory, I presented Greg with his high school Science notebook from the year 1970. The notebook was in his handwriting and very factual and presentable in terms of content and neatness. I had secreted it since Greg had left school and had chosen to present it to him, in front of his family, when Morgan was the same age as Greg at the time that he compiled the notebook. Greg was delighted to peruse the book and more delighted to demonstrate to his children that he had been a 'good student'.

Greg had become acquainted with the game of golf in his mid-teens, and within his first 12 months of playing and of being enamoured of the game I had little support for his pursuit of becoming a professional golfer. I expressed the view at that time that I had observed many trainee professionals and, indeed, qualified professionals who were not financially successful as pros and were therefore facing an insecure future.

Greg's absolute dedication to practice and command of the game, plus the masterly verbal support—which I am sure Greg engineered—by senior qualified professionals whose opinions I respected convinced me to change my mind. From then Greg had our absolute and full support to pursue his desire. The balance of Greg's unfinished golfing career is history.

Some things that I hope to have impressed on Greg during his formative years, and which could generically be herded under the heading of 'philosophies' were:

Never be a 'prima donna' or display such attitudes in any activity in which you are involved.

To be successful in any endeavour the first person you have to have mastery over is yourself.

No self-respecting golfer and, more especially, a professional would ever throw a golf club in anger or disgust.

When considering any action involving other people, consider the consequences of the action on those people.

In a lighter vein, as part of my application of the 'think' aspect of guiding, teaching and cajoling, and during general family conversation, I sometimes quoted extracts from my limited recall of poetry or Shakespeare. One of these was a stanza from a William Cowper poem, 'Boadicea', which I had remembered from my own school days. The particular stanza was:

> *Then the progeny that springs*
> *From the forests of our land,*
> *Armed with thunder, clad with wings,*
> *Shall a wider world command.*

My purpose was to induce in them a subconscious desire to look ahead in life so they could contribute to an increase in their own welfare and to those who would depend on them.

Below: There's room for a young Gregory to fit into the giant silver cup, with a beaming Norman surveying his conquest of the 1986 World Match Play Championship at Wentworth, sponsored by Suntory.

It can be considered that Greg has been in the right place at the right time, with the necessary natural talents and the support of many people. It is significant that he possessed the attitude and dedication to succeed.

He is most fortunate to have met and married Laura. In my opinion, they have an admirable marriage and, as a result of their efforts, a loving and mutually supportive family unit.

Greg's achievements over the past 24-plus years have been well-chronicled by the media and books. My contribution to this book is not licenced to comment on these publications or their contents.

With some satisfaction, I think I can feel that Greg did receive, and act on, my fatherly offerings, subliminal or otherwise.

If this is correct I am a very proud and grateful father to have the pleasure to contribute.

If ever there was an unwritten and unspoken agreement between Greg and me on the way he should pursue and fulfil his life, he receives from me a 100 per cent-plus pass mark for executing his part of that agreement. For my part, I guess that I will continue to be a father.

His mother and I have enjoyed, and continue to receive, compound interest from his endeavours. To us the relationship is precious.

Below: A world sporting celebrity, Norman is most popular in his native state of Queensland. Here he is pictured with wife Laura in 1998 after being presented with an honorary doctorate at Griffith University.
Opposite: One of Greg's second-generation labrador pups, Fosters, introduced into the family in 1991. This pup is now one of four labradors in the Normans' Florida household—each named after an Aussie beer.

Greg has been in the right place at the right time, with the necessary natural talents and the support of many people ... he possessed the attitude and dedication to succeed.

MADNESS AT THE BOTTOM OF A MURKY LAKE

Frank Williams

English-born Frank Williams has an exclusive tale to tell. One of the early two pioneers of the Australian Masters, this whimsical account reveals how a young Greg Norman cheerfully came to their help through early rocky times. The Masters became our greatest tournament success story and Frank Williams was to join the Shark organisation as Norman's business manager. Few know the Shark better.

Having known Greg Norman for some 20-odd years, I look back and the thing that sticks in my mind is how little the substance of the man has changed. He still has the same enthusiasm, ready wit and boyish charm that endeared him to the fans in the 1970s, and that still has the same effect in the 1990s. And apart from being older and wealthier, I genuinely believe nothing has really changed. To quote that well-worn cliché: 'You can take the boy out of Queensland, but you can't take Queensland out of the boy.'

When my ex-partner and I started the Australian Masters, the one person who probably saved us from bankruptcy and public ridicule was Greg Norman. He gave us the credibility, excitement and support that the fledging tournament needed in the late 1970s and early '80s. He heavily promoted the tournament for us and, on many occasions, went over and above what was contractually called for.

For instance, Greg took great delight in doing the promotions associated with the tournament in the early days. And I vividly remember him doing things that seem almost bizarre and impossible for a superstar to undertake in the modern age of sport. In the early days of the Australian Masters we promoted the tournament in the weeks leading up to it by pushing the theme 'The Tradition Continues', and we would enhance this theme with the catchphrase 'Whatever it takes, be there when the tradition continues'. Consequently, we asked Greg to do many promotional activities, like jump out of an airship and sit at the bottom of Huntingdale Lake.

In fact, the story of how we got Greg to emerge from the lake began when I phoned his then manager to ask if Greg would sit at the bottom of the lake with an aqualung, come up from the water holding a five-iron and say to camera, 'Whatever it takes to be

Page 25: The Shark reveals fierce determination even if it is his own sponsored 1991 Shark Shootout tournament he's contesting.
Opposite: The Shark sees a putt shave the cup at the 1991 Johnnie Walker Classic in Sydney.
Left: Norman and caddy pointing to the target at the 1991 Australian Open at Royal Melbourne.
Above: Norman the vibrant competitor at the 1986 British Open.

Below: A serious moment, with Frank Williams and the Shark in earnest conversation at the Australian Golf Club. Right: An exhibition at Huntingdale in 1981. Williams shares a relaxing moment as the Shark waits for traffic ahead to clear. On the far right is Steve Williams, now caddy to Tiger Woods.

Above: The first meeting of Greg Norman and the mighty Jack Nicklaus. Phil Tresidder organised the photograph at the Australian Club, Kensington, on the eve of the 1976 Australian Open, for his newspaper. Norman had just won the West Lakes Classic in Adelaide. Paired with Greg in the opening round, the Golden Bear praised his talented power game.

Opposite: Teenager Gregory Norman Jnr. selects a club under the watchful eye of his proud father at the 1998 Junior Open Championship at Formby. The 'baby shark' is making good progress in the game which has made his father famous.

there, be there when the tradition continues.' Immediately his manager said that we were stark staring mad and refused without hesitation.

Not taking a rebuff kindly, I decided to call Laura Norman and get her opinion on what I thought was a marketing masterpiece. Much to my surprise, she also thought I was mad, but gave me the following advice: If you want Greg to do anything a little out of the ordinary then you have got to relate it to excitement and danger.

So bearing this in mind, I decided to take the bull by the horns and rang Greg at his hotel at a tournament he was playing in the United States, and the following dialogue transpired:

'Hi, Greg. This is Frank. I have this wonderful idea for a promotion for the Australian Masters next year, which I would like you to consider. Do you remember in that James Bond movie how Bond, in a wetsuit and aqualung, swam across the estuary, climbed a wall, blew up Specter's headquarters, swam back to the other side, changed into a dinner jacket and swaggered into the casino after having caused havoc to the enemy? Well, I want you to do something similar to that to promote the golf tournament.'

Greg immediately said, 'Sounds good to me. When do you want to do it?' So it was duly arranged to be shot before the Australian Open in November to be on air during January and February for the lead up to the Australian Masters.

When Greg arrived at Huntingdale in November, the murky waters of Huntingdale Lake on a cold and wet morning bore very little resemblance to James Bond's escapades. But true to his word he donned the wetsuit, sank to the depths of the lake with a rope

Below right: Ever willing to help promoters and sponsors, Norman plays his part here astride a camel and in full Bedouin attire at the 1997 Dubai Desert Classic.
Opposite: Sporting the winning smile as he holds up the trophy at the 1990 Australian Masters at Huntingdale.

tied to his ankle and, when cued by a tug on the rope, emerged from the water and said, 'Whatever it takes to be there, be there when the tradition continues at Huntingdale in February.'

He then came out of the lake, wryly looked me straight in the eye and said, 'Sean Connery never went through this, but I hope it works for you.' To maintain his sense of humour after two hours of getting in and out of the water with calls from the director saying 'Just one more take' showed not only the utmost professionalism, but a true friend doing a favour for a mate.

Consequently, flushed with the success of this promotion, the following year we asked him to get into the Swan Brewery's airship, jump out with a parachute and land on Huntingdale's 18th green, with the now familiar catchphrase: 'Whatever it takes, be there when the tradition continues.' However, after the intervention of his manager's common sense and pleadings from his wife, we did agree to use a stunt double for the actual jump.

But let's make no bones about it. If Greg had had his way, he would have made the jump, and, as he was swaying from a crane at Moorabbin Airport with a parachute attached to his back, those piercing blue eyes looked at me again and he said, 'There's not many people I would do this for, Frank'. I am eternally grateful for what the man was and still is—a good friend.

Greg took great delight in doing the promotions associated with the tournament in the early days. I vividly remember him doing things that seem almost bizarre and impossible for a superstar to undertake in the modern age of sport.

RAPPORT WITH THE SCOTS

by Alex Hay

Alex Hay is the voice of Scotland, the birthplace of the game of golf. BBC commentator, author and general manager of the Woburn Golf Club outside London, Alex Hay, in his rich Scottish brogue, tells how the Scots embraced Greg Norman after his first British Open victory at Turnberry.

That Greg Norman is enormously popular in Scotland goes without question, but why? Is it because he won his first Major, and for some years his only, over the glorious links of Turnberry on the windswept Ayshire coast? Like Tom Watson, who won four Championships on Scottish soil before winning his fifth in England—and therefore became totally accepted by the Scots as one of their own—so it was with Greg.

The Scots also love a fighter, especially one who, though down, battles on. So when Greg arrived at Turnberry in July 1986, having fallen at the final hurdle in both the United States Masters and Open Championships, he found himself with massive local support. This became even more enthusiastic when he compiled one of the finest rounds ever witnessed over the Ailsa Course, a 63 in the second round, played in foul conditions.

Apart from his tenacious style of play, which everyone is thrilled to watch, there is, of course, another side to the man. For even in the heat of competition there are moments when he stops and

Page 35: Norman on the tee and framed by the famous Turnberry lighthouse at the 1986 British Open. A visiting American golfer once asked his Scottish caddie whether the lighthouse still worked. 'Yes, but only at night' came the reply.
Opposite: Greg Norman in full cry is an awesome figure. Here at the 1986 British Open, after a successful stroke, he brandishes his putter in a victory salute that never fails to excite the galleries.
Left: A release of emotions after winning the 1993 British Open.

Above: A thoughtful moment to decide the next move.
Above right: The Shark in full blast during the 1995 US Open at Shinnecock Hills. The Shark led into the last round but faltered, with seasoned campaigner Raymond Floyd taking the prize.

banters with the gallery. At Open Championships, especially in Scotland where the old links were never constructed for arena purposes, the crowds on many occasions are within touching distance of the competitors. Though perhaps not ideal, this feature does provide the perfect stage for Norman who, with that smile of his coupled with a razor-sharp wit, communicates in a very human way which the Scots just love. It is here that the warmth towards the man is easily sensed.

As a BBC television commentator I enjoy the privilege of being able to walk with the players during their practice rounds and I well remember that particular Open. I was so impressed by Greg's play that I walked the entire course with him on both days. I had never before witnessed such confidence nor seen a man so in command

of his game. This I related to the viewing audience on Thursday morning when we went on air, quoting him as my tip to win.

Practising along with Jack Nicklaus and playing so well Greg attracted huge numbers and the atmosphere became extremely relaxed. Going down the fifth, discussion was of a golf course which a friend of Jack's had developed on a small area of land in the Caymen Islands. Because the course was so short Jack had produced a ball that only travelled exactly half the distance of a normal one. In this way all you had to do was double the actual distance before you select the appropriate club, then the ball would do the rest. This was verified when Jack produced from his bag one of the balls and, as you would expect, Greg just had to try it out.

The sixth at Turnberry is a par three from an elevated tee measuring 222 yards, where large numbers gather to enjoy a testing tee shot. The players were welcomed with much enthusiasm and, like most who had already played through, Big Jack—as he is affectionately known in those parts, having also won his first Open on Scottish soil 20 years before—selected a long iron and punched a beautiful shot to the heart of the green. A stunned silence fell over the crowd when the mighty Australian pulled the headcover off his driver. The disbelief continued when what sounded like a perfect strike resulted in the ball falling into the valley some 50 yards short of the green. Then to cap, Jack announced, 'You'll need a good eight-iron from there!'

Greg proceeded to play the next three holes using the ball for a wager and betting that he could play them in less than 15 shots. I am fairly certain that the gradually depleting numbers witnessing this exhibition, but knowing nothing of the ball in use, must surely have wondered how this man, who could barely reach the fairways with his drives, would go on to win his first Open Championship. Nevertheless, Greg did win the bet, but only just.

Much to my own pleasure I am happy to report that Greg does not win all of his bets. Almost 12 months after his victory I received a telephone call from him. Could he and his great chum, Nigel

Mansell, come and play nine holes at Woburn when the qualifying laps for the British Grand Prix were completed at Silverstone? This was the week before Greg would defend his title so I was delighted that our Open champion would visit the Club where I was Director and where he had won the Dunlop Masters title in 1981.

The pair duly flew in, much to the pleasure of Club members who witnessed their arrival by helicopter, having only just viewed the time trials on the Club's television. 'C'mon, Alex, you can play too! I'll take on the pair of you for a fiver.'

Having never played against a current Open Champion I was, to say the least, just a little nervous and well aware of my inadequacies as I attempted to tee up the ball with trembling fingers. Praying that I might get it off the peg, I somehow managed to hit the best drive I can ever recall. Off it soared, straight down the middle. I turned to Greg, beaming with pride, whereupon he tossed me a ball. 'Hard luck; have a mulligan!'

I managed to halve the first three holes; then Nigel, with the help of a couple of strokes and a gross eagle, took us into a winning position and Greg reached for his wallet. 'No Greg, not here; wait until we're in front of the clubhouse windows'.

With his perfect timing, just as we passed the bar he called us over and produced two crisp five pound notes and paid up. What

Above left: Even in the heat of British Open battle there's always a moment to relax. The Shark stretches out to take it all in during the final round at the 1986 British Open, perhaps sniffing the victory ahead.
Above: The 1986 Open Championship trophy, the auld claret jug, is held up by Greg Norman and wife Laura after his five-shot victory.

a moment that was for me, and I have noticed that Nigel refers to it more often than he does the British Grand Prix where he stormed to victory next day. My members certainly treated me with more respect from then on.

In 1989, at Royal Troon, the Scottish hearts went out to their Australian hero when, after a blistering final round of 64 and yet another course record, he had made it into the play-off—only to lose on the 18th when his aggressive play was to cost him the victory that seemed in his grasp. His mighty drive made it to a bunker which the Club committee had debated removing. The new Championship tee had, it was felt, rendered that bunker so far out of range that it was now superfluous. How unfortunate it hadn't gone at the time the tee was built.

Again, in 1990 at St. Andrews, Greg's Scottish fans suffered with him. After two brilliant rounds of 66 he matched Nick Faldo's 67 and 65 only to collapse with a 76, while the Englishman scored 67. But three years later at Royal St. George's, Greg found sweet revenge. This golfer who is sometimes down but never out was in complete command and his magnificent final round of 64 overtook the overnight leader, Nick Faldo, and gave Greg his second Open Championship.

What a pity he did it in England.

Below: The Shark searches for an opening through the trees after a wayward shot in the 1998 Australian Open, Royal Adelaide Golf Course. Opposite: A shock of thatch-coloured hair, waves breaking on the rocks and the Turnberry lighthouse in the background—the 1986 British Open.

Apart from his tenacious style of play, which everyone is thrilled to watch, there is, of course, another side to the man. For even in the heat of competition there are moments when he stops and banters with the gallery.

THE HARMON YEARS

by Bruce Critchley

In his day a British Walker Cup golfer, Bruce Critchley is now one of the game's most incisive commentators—both authoritative and entertaining. For many years with BBC Television, he has, more recently, been commentating with B Sky B. Also a self-author, in this contribution he recaptures the week in which 'while the perfect golfer is yet to emerge, Norman was damn close to it'.

'I think Greg Norman is one of the truly great players the game has ever seen.' These are the words of Butch Harmon, Norman's guide and mentor in the early 1990s and, more recently, coach to Tiger Woods.

'I was always intrigued by Greg's ability to shoot low numbers,' Harmon goes on, 'his ability to handle the slings and arrows so well, and his will to get back up there into the fray despite the knocks. I had studied his swing a lot, as I have all the great players, and I was well prepared if the time ever came we should get together.'

That time came towards the end of 1991. The Houston Open that year had been postponed due to bad weather. Harmon lived in Houston, and, on the advice of Steve Elkington, Norman sought him out. Norman was in the one prolonged slump of his golfing life. He had not won for more than a year and, more seriously, was squandering dominant positions in ordinary tour events that, in the past, he'd harvested like a farmer making hay.

The Western Open at Cog Hill, Illinois was a case in point. Comfortably in front with nine to play, Norman scattered shots all

Page 45: Safely on the green, the Shark removes his glove for the all-important putt, the stage where tournaments are won or lost.
Opposite: Norman takes to the microphone at his own tournament, the Greg Norman Holden Classic, the Australian Golf Club, in 1997.
Below: Norman exchanges greetings with the great Arnold Palmer. Many saw the Shark as Palmer's future successor.

Above: Norman receives congratulations at the 1986 Queensland Open at Tweed Heads from a long-standing admirer, Stefan, the Queensland hairdressing king and sponsor of the Queensland Open. Opposite: Enchanting daughter Morgan-Leigh views her father's handiwork in beating Sandy Lyle in the final of the 1983 World Match Play Championship.

over the final few holes to let in left-handed journeyman Russ Cochran. Earlier in the year he had wilted against Peter Senior in the home straight of the Australian Masters, a tournament at which, in the past, his sheer presence at the top of the leader board would have brought on an attack of the vapours in his nearest challengers.

The cause of this fallibility can be traced back to the previous year's British Open at St. Andrews. Nick Faldo was at the peak of his career, having just won the US Masters and being one short putt away from a play-off for the US Open. Even so, he had had to give best to Norman in February at Huntingdale, where they had gone head to head over the final two rounds in the Australian Masters. Norman had also shown impressive form in America, winning twice and taming Doral's Blue Monster with an astonishing 62 in the final round.

St. Andrews was the perfect setting for the year's great duel, and when they shared the lead after two rounds, four ahead of the rest, it was Huntingdale revisited. But on the very first hole of the third round a pattern was established. With both players some 25 feet from the hole in two, Faldo putted first and holed. Norman missed, and while Faldo sailed away to a majestic 67, Norman slowly came apart to finish nine shots behind.

In the past, Norman had shown enormous resilience to shrug off high-profile golfing calamities; some of his own doing, some at the hands of others. Each time he had bounced back, his passion for limelight and glory undimmed by agonising failure. That was until St. Andrews. Maybe it was the day-long slide from grace; the full 18-hole humiliation. This time Norman did not recover, at least not on his own.

'When we first spoke, Greg was no longer doing many of the things that had made him a great player,' Harmon recalls. 'He seemed lost in the way he was swinging. All I did then was make a few suggestions that got him back on track and he began to play well again.' With trust established between them, Norman was prepared to listen further to Harmon.

Norman's Achilles heel had long been that blocked shot to the

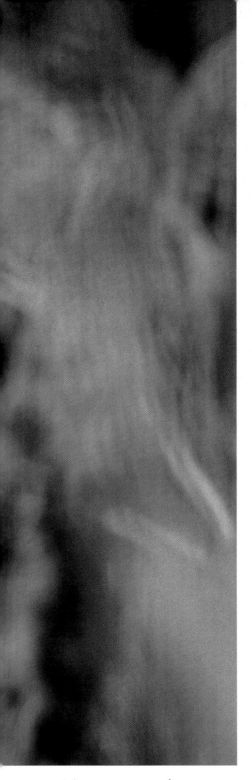

right at moments of supreme stress. The 72nd hole at Winged Foot in the 1984 US Open comes to mind, as does the final hole at Augusta two years later.

'For a tall man, his stance was too narrow,' was the Harmon analysis. 'With a full swing, his weight was all on the left side. To get back to the ball he had to get out of his own way and that meant a big slide of the hips and that trademark backward slip of the right foot. Only great last-minute adjustments with his hands had enabled him to play so well so often.'

The stance was widened, the hips made to rotate rather than tilt, and the swing became wider and shorter; changes scarcely noticeable to the naked eye, but most significant to a golfer in his mid-thirties who had been swinging one way all his life.

The changes were similar to those Nick Faldo had worked on

Above left: Norman's career has taken him far and wide across the globe. He is wearing Australasian colours, playing against South Africa at the Houghton Club, Johannseburg in 1995.
Above: The 1993 Heineken Australian Open was hard work in the heat and a cool drink is a much-needed reviver.

in the mid-1980s, which had taken him a full three years to perfect. But for Norman it was at the British Open of the following year, just nine months on, that he began to feel comfortable.

It was now more than two years since he had won anything, but in September of that year he had a chance to see if he still knew how. The answer would be yes. Despite a stumbling final few holes, Greg won the Canadian Open in a play-off with Bruce Lietzke. A vital hurdle had been crossed.

The following spring he swept away a top-class field in the Doral Ryder Open, beating its previous 72-hole record by five shots. Norman was now as good as before—but was he better?

Once more, the British Open was the acid test. With a round to go at Royal St. George's, the cream of world golf was in contention. Faldo, the defending champion, was in the lead, but Norman overtook him with two birdies in the first three holes. And while Fred Couples, Nick Price, Ernie Els and Corey Pavin failed to last the pace, the final nine holes became an epic battle between Norman, Faldo and Bernhard Langer.

Norman was never caught, and in the process broke all sorts of records with a final round of 64. If ever he was going to crack, to hit one of those wild destructive shots at a crucial moment, it would be with the likes of Faldo and Langer at their peak, breathing down his neck. Norman never wavered. The perfect golfer is yet to emerge, but that day Norman was damn close to it.

Below: Butch Harmon (second from right) has an attentive audience with (from left) Nick Price, Raymond Floyd and the Shark.
Opposite: Norman in firm control of the British Open trophy in 1993, Royal St. George's.

Norman had shown enormous resilience to shrug off high-profile calamaties; some of his own doing, some at the hands of others. Each time he has bounced back, his passion for limelight and glory undimmed by agonising failure.

A CARING PERSON

by Richie Benaud

Richie Benaud was one of the all-time, great cricket leaders—never defeated in a Test series—and one of the game's finest all-rounders. But by choice, he is never happier than when involved in the golf scene; and his respect for, and association with Greg Norman has seen Richie and wife Daphne make annual pilgrimages to Augusta to follow the Shark's fortunes. This is one legend's tribute to another.

t is close to a quarter of a century since I first watched Greg Norman play golf, a sighting at the behest, or really far more under instruction, from Peter Thomson who was walking with him at the Grange course in Adelaide where the West Lakes Classic was being played and Norman was 'streeting' his rivals.

I was working in the media tent with my wife, Daphne, when 'Thommo' arrived and said to both of us, 'You've always claimed you want to be there at the start of someone's career, so whatever you're doing now, drop it. I want you to come with me over the final holes and see this young Norman win the tournament, because he's going to be one of the great players the world has seen. And then you can say you were there when it all began.'

I've always been grateful that we walked the last few holes of that event with Peter. It gave us the introduction to much of Greg's golf over the years.

Page 55: An Aussie triumph. Norman and Steve Elkington embrace after taking out the Shark's own shootout at Sherwood Country Club in 1998.
Opposite: A renowned traveller worldwide, Norman peers between the palm fronds at the 1991 Johnnie Walker World Championship at the Tryall Resort in the Caribbean. He finished tied fourth.
Below: Norman gets a pat on the back from the golfer he admires most, Jack Nicklaus.

Left: Camera catches the drama so often associated with a Greg Norman recovery adventure—in this case at the 1996 Heineken Classic.
Above: A congratulatory hug from wife Laura.

For me, along with Seve Ballesteros, he has been the most exciting player I've watched. This was only Norman's third professional tournament and he won nothing more that year, nor in 1977 and we read of his progress rather than watched it. When we saw him in Adelaide that day he was blond, tall and broad-shouldered, and looked exactly what he was: a surfer-cum-footballer who had decided to take up golf because he thought his mother made it look so easy when she played.

We began covering the Masters Tournament at Augusta in 1979 when Fuzzy Zoeller won in a play-off, then watched Seve Ballesteros beat Gibby Gilbert and Jack Newton in 1980. Norman wasn't invited to Augusta that year but when he won the Australian Open late in 1980 the invitation for 1981 arrived a couple of months later and we were there to watch him.

It remains one of the great experiences of my sporting life to have walked the final 18 holes of that tournament with Tom Watson, the eventual winner, and Norman, who finished fourth, with Johnny Miller and Jack Nicklaus second and third respectively. Norman, David Graham and Newton were the only Australian representatives in that event.

Above: Richie Benaud no slouch himself on the golf course. Here he is pictured at the 1983 Bob Hope Classic.
Right: Down but not out. Norman slips at the feet of Nicklaus in the 1986 World Match Play.

Unwittingly, during the media conference at the end of the third round, Norman was caught up in some controversy. Nicklaus and Watson had assumed—and hoped—they would be head-to-head on the final day. However, they had forgotten that at Augusta the leader of the third round—Watson, in this case—would play with Norman and the second-placed Nicklaus would be with number four—John Mahaffey. It was information received with dismay by the two stars, equanimity by Norman, who didn't mind what the draw produced.

In the end, it turned out to be just one of those rounds for Norman with four birdies, four bogeys and no birdies on the par fives, but it was enough. As television viewers, we went through the ensuing sagas with Zoeller at Winged Foot in 1984 and Bob Tway at Inverness in 1986. We were there for the 1986 Masters when Nicklaus's surge to victory was one of the most exciting things imaginable, even if you happened to be cheering for Norman. Daph and I were getting close to filing time for morning newspapers in Australia and we decided I should wait for Nicklaus at the 17th green and Daph would go with Greg and Nicky Price who were now just about to hit off on fifteen.

Suddenly up came the scoreboards around the course with news of Nicklaus's birdie on the par-three 16th. The 2000 spectators cramming and cheering around Norman and Price disappeared, all racing for the 17th fairway vantage points. Daph, standing next to Greg, got the quote of the day which I used as my intro: 'Come on Nicky, let's show these bastards we can play golf'.

Above: Like a Red Indian scout on the lookout, Norman surveys the scene for his next adventure.

61

Below: Laura and daughter Morgan-Leigh are Norman's best supporters. Here, with a friend, they take an advantage point with the action below.
Opposite: A look into the future at the 1993 Johnnie Walker Classic.

I'm sorry to have to tell that, after the Melbourne *Herald* sub-editor's desk had a mild panic attack, it appeared in far more staid terms, just like an intro for the *Church Times*.

Staying at the 17th as I did gave me the chance to see a memorable putt after Nicklaus had hit his pitch shot to around 12 to 14 feet. I was then able to position myself behind the hole. It was a putt that broke to Nicklaus's right and then immediately back to the left. I then heard one of the greatest roars of my time produced from a crowd.

It was the same two people, Norman and Nicklaus, who provided us with one of the greatest moments off the course. It was at Turnberry in 1986, after the Nicklaus Masters win, and on the third evening Greg and Laura invited Daph and me to dinner in the Turnberry Hotel. In the second round I had followed Norman when he shot an astonishing 63 which included three bogeys, and that in difficult weather conditions. The third day brought appalling weather, a fierce south-westerly wind and torrential rain for most of the way around. Norman's 74 was good enough to give him a one-stroke lead, on 211, as we sat down to dinner.

It was during the dinner that Nicklaus came and sat alongside and slightly behind Norman and, in one of the more fascinating events I have witnessed, I watched the two of them working their hands, simulating the gripping action on an imaginary club. Nicklaus was offering advice in a chatty way about relaxed hands under pressure on the basis that he mightn't see much of Norman the following day since 16 shots separated them on the pairing sheet.

Norman won his first major the next day and you can bet your life the relaxed hands lesson during that dinner had something to do with it. It had been an evening to remember, and this victory a day to remember.

In my view, Greg Norman is one of the greatest sportsmen to represent Australia and has been, over the years, a wonderful inspiration to youngsters all over the nation. He has provided a great boost to the game of golf and continues to do so, not least with his comeback in 1999 at the age of 44, after a serious shoulder operation, to play with such skill and temperament to claim fourth place behind Jose Maria Olazabal at the Masters.

More than any of Norman's victories though, two things will stay in my mind about the Augusta Tournament. The first was on the 485-yard 13th hole where Norman hit a four-iron to 25 feet and sank the putt for eagle. Then Olazabal sank a wonderful 18-footer for birdie and they were both grinning at the other and pointing a finger of congratulations. There was also the fact that each man had come back from injuries so serious they might never have played again, and they said they had kept in touch during their more unhappy times and that 'he' was a caring person.

He was blond, tall and broad-shouldered, and looked exactly what he was: a surfer-cum-footballer who had decided to take up golf because he thought his mother made it look so easy ...

ROUTING THE PUNY CRITICS

by Bob Hawke

Australia's longest-serving Labor Prime Minister (four terms: 1983–1991), President of the Australian Council of Trade Unions (1970–1980), WA Rhodes Scholar (1953) and passionate sports lover, Bob Hawke treasures his frequent appearances with Greg Norman as his partner in pro-am events. He is angered by some of the churlish criticism levelled at the Shark over the years and takes these critics sternly to task in this Norman tribute.

No Australian sportsman or sportswoman in the second half of this century has done more to advance the image of their sport and their country than Gregory John Norman.

Greg has inspired countless thousands of the young—and not so young—to take up the frustrating but ultimately rewarding game of golf. He has been the role model for so many of our young stars, male and female, who have gone on to make their mark in this fiercely competitive sport.

Greg's impact is not due simply to his magnificent record of achievement, but also to the vitality and integrity, and the commitment to fair play that he has brought to the game at all times. No one wants to win more than Greg, but winning at all costs is not part of his philosophy. Some sportsmen and sportswomen are single-minded in the pursuit of victory, but Greg has never forgotten the traditions and proper code of behaviour of the game. He has consistently demonstrated to the world the best Australian characteristics, as perceived by Australians—directness tinged with brashness; self-confidence; respect for others, regardless of colour, race or creed; a sense of 'the fair thing'; and, as I will elaborate later, a genuine compassion for those less fortunate than himself.

And yet, paradoxically, he has been the victim of an Australian characteristic which, when taken to extremes, can be unattractive

Page 65: The 1993 British Open at Royal St George's and the Shark muscles a recovery shot out of the rough on his way to his second British Open Victory.
Opposite: Norman is king again, this time at Kapalua, Hawaii in 1983 with his shining prize.
Below: A moment of success at Augusta in 1999 ... but the Masters prize eluded him.

Below: Bob Hawke and Greg Norman, frequent pro-am partners over the years, discuss club selection.
Opposite: The craggy profile of the Shark. An American critic once wrote he could pass for a light heavyweight boxer in any bar in the world. Here he is pictured at the 1995 Johnnie Walker Classic in Manila.

and hurtful: the tall poppy syndrome. The egalitarian impulse in our society is admirable, but it assumes an ugly face when the mean-minded use any instrument to cut down those who, by their genuine achievements, come to tower above other mere mortals, as Greg has done.

The paradox is compounded by the fact that these detractors latch upon the very traits of the Australian character we all admire—the directness, the brashness, the self-confidence, the will to succeed—and then exaggerate and distort them into a parody of the real man. Greg Norman, more than any other illustrious Australian sportsman, has been the undeserved victim of these mindless vultures. And what annoys them more than anything else is that Greg won't lie down and die and give them the satisfaction of picking over the carcass.

They have called Greg's self-confidence arrogance and have made these accusations without foundation as I can attest, better than most, from my intimate knowledge of, and friendship with him. Greg does have an enormous and thoroughly justified pride in his achievements in the world of golf and business. He is well aware that they are a finely honed combination of a rare natural talent, dedication, a commitment to practice and sheer hard work. To speak with a self-confidence fuelled by his merits is not arrogance. And no-one is more qualified to speak with authority about the game.

Opposite: A neat trick, balancing the ball on the open blade of a sandwedge. Norman shows his sleight-of-hand after holing out from a bunker in the 1989 International at Castle Pines Golf Club, Colorado.
Above: Greg tilts with a nasty pot bunker at the 1996 British Open at Royal Lytham & St Annes Golf Club.

Another part of the paradox is that the magnitude of Greg's achievements is used by some of his knockers to denigrate the man. He has won so many times against the world's best that they seize upon the number of his near-misses in the majors and label him a 'choker'. The simple fact is that if he were not the great player he is, Greg would not have put himself in a potentially winning position. He has been the victim of cruel misfortune and, on occasion, as Greg is the first to admit, less than perfect club selection or shot execution. But as Pope put it: 'To err is human, to forgive, divine', and I'm sure that the Almighty, like Greg Norman's host of admirers around the world, has forgiven Greg any such errors in assessing the balance of his outstanding record.

And, for me, it is the conduct of this fallible human being on these heart-rending occasions that gives Greg the real stamp of greatness. How can anyone who has witnessed his courage, composure and supreme good sportsmanship at these times begin to question his enormous strength of character. These qualities were again displayed when he came so close to winning the 1999 Masters title after coming back from extensive shoulder surgery.

As he so richly deserves, Greg has prospered from his power on the golf course in his expanding business interests. Some of his puny critics who even seem to begrudge him his wealth would do well to spend a little time thinking, and writing, about his many good works. Among numerous charitable activities Greg has for many years assisted the National Childhood Cancer Foundation and the Royal Melbourne Children's Hospital.

But to give you the measure of the man, let me share this direct personal experience. Greg agreed to my request, as Chairman of the Sydney City Mission Fund Raising Task Force, to appear as guest of honour at our Appeal Dinner on a Monday night in December 1998.

He had flown from the Australian Open in Adelaide on the Sunday evening to Brisbane for business commitments on Monday, and had to be up early on the Tuesday morning in Melbourne for team practice for the Presidents Cup. He flew into Sydney at about eight on the Monday evening and gave so generously of his time, against the worried urgings to depart by some of his entourage, that his flight was diverted from Essendon to Tullamarine. When I suggested that an auction item of a round of golf with him at his Florida course would raise a few dollars he said, 'Let's make it two'. That item went for $62,000 and helped to augment the amount raised on that evening to $600,000— most of which was due to Greg's attendance. Don't let anyone say anything against Greg Norman in my hearing.

I salute Greg—a good man, one of the greatest golfers of all time and a marvellous ambassador for Australia, the country he still calls home.

... he has been the victim of an Australian characteristic which, when taken to extremes, can be unattractive and hurtful: the tall poppy syndrome.

THE MAN WHO'S GOT EVERYTHING

by Ian Wooldridge

World title fights, Olympics, Test matches ... Ian Wooldridge, the London Daily Mail chief sports columnist, is the man on the spot at the world's most prestigious events. He has even participated in the events he writes about, such as having ridden a husky snow sled across Alaska and taken on the Cresta run on a toboggan. He has joined the Augusta galleries to cheer on Greg Norman and tags him 'The Man Who's Got Everything'.

After five vain attempts to extricate his ball from a pot bunker at St. Andrews many years ago, an exasperated Bernard Darwin, the most elegant of all golf writers, was seen to look skyward and mutter, 'Help me, God, and don't send the lad. You'd better come yourself.'

Darwin's supplication came to mind as Greg Norman faced the press after losing to Jose Maria Olazabal in the 1999 US Masters at Augusta. We had, of course, all been present in 1996 when Greg blew a six-shot last-day advantage to lose to Nick Faldo.

On that occasion, 'The Man Who's Got Everything'—enough to set up his great-grandchildren for life—made a remarkable human gesture. By his side at the podium, presiding over the press conference, was an Augusta National member adorned in the Green Jacket of this most exclusive golf club in the world. A professional golfer can slip into one only by winning the Masters.

At one juncture, Greg leaned across and held the official's right lapel between first finger and thumb. 'Yeah,' he said, 'but I haven't got one of these. And Nick's got three.'

The pain was palpable. Three years later it was less evident, and by 1999 there was a touch of resignation. He had fought out a thrilling battle, toe-to-toe, hole by hole, in what was virtually a match-play head-to-head. But he had lost again.

Thus Bernard Darwin's prayer came flooding back because at this point, it seemed, only someone-up-there could determine whether Greg Norman would win the title he craves more than any

Page 75: A moment's meditation, in 1992, amid the life of the man who 'spends much of his enviable life on the cutting edge of a supersonic track'.
Opposite: Norman negotiates a bush as an added hazard in the 1991 British Open.
Below: Can't believe it! Golf, like life, wasn't meant to be easy.

Below: His parents say he's strictly non-musical but the Shark takes on the trumpeter's role in this 1986 fairway scene.
Opposite: Greg is interrogated after losing another major—the 1996 US Masters at Augusta National.

other. He's had his chances—three big ones, actually—but the years are running out.

It's all comparative, of course. I do not belong to that school of sports-writing which sees triumph and disaster at each end of the spectrum. Triumph is discovering penicillin; disaster is the Balkans. Losing—even winning—a major golf championship is trivial in comparison but, in big sport, to meet either of Kipling's twin imposters with modesty in victory or dignity in defeat are admirable characteristics.

I have seen Greg Norman do both: at Turnberry in 1986, when he won the British Open Championship, and at Augusta, in both 1996 and 1999, when he was within touching distance of the great prize and each time failed to grasp it.

The measure of a man, they say, is grace under pressure. The measure of a great man is grace under crushing disappointment, and if the Augusta National awarded green jackets for that, Greg Norman would already have two.

In 1999 he was almost philosophical. In 1996 he was less so. He was so in command on the final morning that on meeting him outside the locker room, Peter Dobereiner, a friend and irreverent British journalist, said, 'Listen, Greg, even you can't screw this one up.'

Faldo wound in those six shots to beat him and what followed, in front of 300 reporters, was the most extraordinary press conference I have attended. Greg arrived, hollow-eyed and expressionless, and it was an age before anyone braved a question.

Eventually someone asked, 'What happened, Greg?'

'I played like shit,' replied Norman, 'that's what happened.'

This may well strike you as excessive vulgarity but it was out of his system. What followed was firstly generous acclaim for Faldo's near-immaculate golf on the day and then an accurate appraisal of what happened. I still have my notes.

'That's golf,' said Norman. 'I played three rounds just about as well as I could have played them. I didn't wake up feeling any particular tension. I went through the usual routine and I was feeling pretty good. Then I went out there and it was all gone. When if I'd played half-decently it would have been a great tussle. But I didn't.'

No excuses; no sentiment from the man statistically rated at the time as the greatest golfer in the world. Just reality about the exacting demands of a sport which, financially, has launched him beyond the bounds of a golf course into a far wider world.

'No,' he said, 'I shan't secretly creep off to my room and bash my head against the wall. I'm a winner. I've won plenty of golf

Left: More fierce adventure from the 'man of action'.
Below: The Shark image is colourfully inscribed on the Greg Norman International Trophy, a prize on the 1998 Australasian Tour.

tournaments. Winning is about what you put into it. If I'd wanted to be a brain surgeon I'd have been a good one. I just didn't get the job done here, that's all. But I have a pretty good life and it's not the end of the world.'

He was questioned for a captivating half hour. Only occasionally was he interrupted by those on the lower rung of American journalism—which is about as dumb as it gets—to recall which irons he'd hit at such-and-such a hole. Each time he responded with patient courtesy, realising that they'd entirely missed the point.

The entire point of his bravura that evening came in a single sentence: 'I'm a golfer, a man who hits a ball from A to B, and I've created something out of absolutely nothing.'

Created something out of absolutely nothing. It was not a modest remark but Greg Norman is not a modest man. He has no cause to be. But some day, long delayed I trust, it will make a striking epitaph.

Few star sportsmen will have the wit to acknowledge the truth of it. Even fewer will understand the inspiration it can bring to kids, from ghettoes and broken homes and the hinterlands of Queensland, who aspire to follow in their footsteps.

The message is simple: 'If I can do it, so can you.' Greg Norman said it off the cuff. It should be preserved in the aphorisms of sporting literature.

Below: Tournament golf can become a trial of patience. It's go-slow up ahead and Greg Norman and Tom Watson share relaxing moments on the tee.
Opposite: Norman silhouetted against the sun, pushing through a hot, hazy sky at the Emirates Club, Dubai, in the 1997 Desert Classic.

The entire part of his bravura that evening came in a single sentence: 'I'm a golfer, a man who hits a ball from A to B, and I've created something out of absolutely nothing.' Greg Norman said it off the cuff. It should be preserved in the aphorisms of sporting literature.

FULL-THROTTLE LIFESTYLE

by Kaye Kessler

Bombed out of four London sites during World War II while performing duties with American and British intelligence, Kaye Kessler has since discovered more peaceful pastures in the roles of columnist, sportswriter and players' relation director in golf. A president of the Golf Writers Association of America, he is a distinguished figure among the American press gallery and a warm admirer of the Shark, whom he describes as 'the most intimidating golfer in the game today'.

Page 85: Norman punches the air in triumph after holing a chip shot after the 1995 World Series at Akron, Ohio.
These pages, clockwise from top left: Greg Norman's Sydney store sells exclusively the Great White Shark golfwear. Greg Norman is tagged the all-action man. No wonder—the camera catches him sprinting from his helicoper, and a shot of his monster luxury super yacht.

n today's fantasy world, he's everyone's idol, every man's dream, could be Romeo to all Juliets. This is an enigmatic Adonis who consorts with presidents, flies with the angels, drives with the demons, swims with sharks, sails with the wind and laughs at the odds. He's spent much of his enviable life on the cutting edge of a supersonic track and has suddenly come to peace with himself, short, maybe, of goals set by others.

He's Gregory John Norman, the multi-talented Shark with a major appetite; an appetite he has sated with perhaps everything but the collection of 'major' trophies for which everyone figured he was so marvellously suited.

What Norman may be, however, above all else, is the best loser the game has ever known—next to the Golden Bear, Jack Nicklaus—and the man, for so many years, thought of as 'Bear-apparent' to the title of the next-best golfer of all time.

Now that the game's most recent wunderkind, Tiger Woods, has come down to earth and been proven mortal, it can be said that the Shark, once again, is the most intimidating golfer in the game today, who does not have his trophy case filled with major baubles.

At the age of 44, and despite being freshly repaired from shoulder problems which derailed him during virtually all of 1998, it becomes more and more doubtful that Norman will ever achieve major immortality. Still, it can now be safely said that Norman has made peace with himself about his position in golf and life, that

never has there been a more popular foreign golfer on American soil than the effervescent Shark.

The foreign invasion on the US Tour has been ample and impressive, dating back to South African Bobby Locke after World War II. A virtual armada of foreign golfers have left their cleek marks on the US PGA Tour and gained great favour, from the irrepressible Gary Player and Roberto De Vicenzo to Seve Ballesteros, Nick Faldo and Nick Price. Today, there is the influx of awesome alien challenges from the likes of Ernie Els, Vijay Singh, Steve Elkington and Jesper Parnevik.

None had the swagger, the pizazz, the personality, the presence and talent to match the swashbuckling Australian Shark. None, maybe until Tiger, had the magnetism to attract the galleries, save tournaments or generate electricity in an event like Norman. For all of his Pepsodent smile, his 21 US Tour victories and his effusiveness, Player could not generate a buzz in the galleries like Norman. For all of his Latin charm and tree-rattling circus-like recovery theatrics, Ballesteros never captivated US audiences on and off the course like Norman.

Unlike any other foreign golfer, Norman has also endured the

Above: Ready to pounce, the Shark surveys his next challenge in the 1988 Australian Open at Royal Sydney.
Right: The shining silver trophy telling the story of another of his Australian Open successes.
Opposite: Norman and the Golden Bear on the tee. As a schoolboy, Norman secreted a Jack Nicklaus instructional golfing book under his school desk.

Above: The Shark parades his prize after winning the high altitude 1989 International at Castle Pines, Colorado.

challenges, dares and stares, and won the friendship of US golfers themselves—a testimony to his personality and talent. If he ever has been held at arm's length by his fellow golfers, it is because of his full-throttle lifestyle and not his ability to relate to them.

Jack Nicklaus may figure on the all-time money list behind even Chip Beck, but he owns 18 professional majors among his 70 Tour and 14 international titles. Sam Snead, with an all-time high of 81 Tour victories, had career earnings of just $US620,126, which is about $US280,000 less than the sum David Duval received for winning the 1999 Players' Championship.

The cold, hard truth is that Norman has gained greater stature and considerably wider popularity in the United States for the way he has handled adversity about 'the ones that got away' than for any of his 18 US Tour victories.

Again, Greg has captivated more fan favour for his losses than his only two major triumphs in the British Open, gaining a most favourable comparison with Nicklaus who is universally credited with being an even better loser than a winner. Case in point: Nicklaus has 70 Tour wins and 58 second places. He has won 18 pro majors and was second 18 times. Greg's 18 Tour wins are followed by 31 second places. And while he has just the two British Open titles, he's better remembered for eight runner-ups in the majors.

Maybe it's the manner in which Greg has been denied. He squandered a huge lead in losing the 1996 Masters to Faldo, was victimised by Larry Mize's 160-foot chip-in on the second play-off hole of the 1987 Masters, and lost to Nicklaus by two the year before. He lost the 1984 US Open in a play-off with Fuzzy Zoeller and the 1995 Open to Corey Pavin, lost the 1986 PGA when Bob Tway blasted into the cup from a bunker on the last hole and lost the 1993 PGA in a play-off with Paul Azinger.

This is a star-crossed man with the world by the tail. A man with an animal magnetism that makes him as commercially attractive as Michael Jordan, Nicklaus or Palmer if he never strikes another golf ball. His personal toys include a new 158-foot yacht named Aussie Rules, which made its maiden voyage to Hilton Head the week after the Masters; a new 61-foot sportfisher he calls The Medallist; a Gulfstream V jet plane and more sport automobiles than most dealers. He is in great demand as a golf course architect and has a wife and two children to die for—which he insists are now the focal point of his life.

Still, fans actually wept for Norman at Augusta when his latest bid for a coveted Green Masters Jacket was thwarted by Spaniard Jose Maria Olazabal's gutsy finish. Cheers for Greg from spectators as he went toe-to-toe the final 18 holes with Olazabal were chilling, reaching the proportions of reverence shown for Nicklaus in his stunning final nine holes to win the 1986 Masters and almost

Below: Norman is a popular figure in the Florida scene, pictured here flexing a baseball bat in the company of two Miami Dolphin baseballers.

as deafening as the cheers when Ben Hogan played his incredible back nine 30 on the Saturday of his last Masters in 1967.

The Masters has become Norman's Achilles heel. Yet in his most recent disappointment he emerged even more golden. As *Golf Week*'s Brian Hewitt wrote: 'Jose won, but the Shark got everybody's attention—sympathy, cheers, love and admiration.'

Golf World's Bob Verdi wrote: 'The more he loses at the wire, the more he wins at public opinion polls. If body English could push an Australian to the victory he so craves, he'd have lapped the field.'

Many perceived the Shark a kinder, gentler, more compassionate man as he hugged Olazabal on the 18th green, and spoke of their friendship and how they had rooted for each other in their dark moments of recovery in the past three years.

Players have aligned themselves with Norman. Price stopped to applaud on the 18th green as he heard the cheers for Norman's eagle back at 13. Davis Love III, second and a shot ahead of Norman at the finish, offered the Shark condolences in the locker-room, adding, 'We'll both get one eventually.' And Duval, currently holding the world No. 1 ranking that seemed Norman's province for so many years, said, 'I don't think anybody ever is owed anything, but you know, with all the heartache he has had here, if I can't pull it off, it wouldn't kill me to see him do it.'

Below: A precious addition to the Greg Norman photo album as he shakes hands with Gene Sarazen, one of golf's all-time legends, during the 1993 US PGA Championship.
Opposite: A cheery smile but no trophy for the Shark at the 1991 Australian Open, Royal Melbourne.

None had the swagger, the pizazz, the personality, the presence and talent to match the swashbuckling Australian Shark. None had the magnetism to attract the galleries, save tournaments or generate electricity in an event like Norman.

THE GOLF IS ON!

by Allan Border

Even sporting champions themselves have their own heroes. Allan Border, cricket's prolific run-getter and triumphant Test captain, found inspiration from Greg Norman as their respective careers dovetailed. Border's tribute reflects the strong affinity that exists between golf and cricket.

Greg Norman has been an inspiration to me throughout my career. We are the same age and started our respective careers at approximately the same time.

I can distinctly remember watching this strapping young golfer—who looked as if he would be just at home on a surfboard as on a golf course—win the Westlakes Classic in 1976. I was immediately impressed.

Not long after, I started playing Test cricket for Australia. Even way back then there was something very special about Greg. He had presence and charisma, and he could really hit that ball.

Over the ensuing years I've related very closely to Greg's success and his failures. Our sports are different, but the efforts that go into training and practice, the strive for excellence, and the incredible highs—as well as the desperate lows—are things we both have experienced. I can appreciate how Greg feels and, personally, I think he has done a wonderful job.

Most cricketers are avid golfers as well as spectators of the sport, particularly on television, and it has been through television

Page 95: A copybook finish to the power-house swing of Norman, one of the game's biggest hitters.

Opposite: The Shark power game in full throttle at the 1989 International at Castle Pines, Colorado. Norman won this US PGA event.

Below: There are few better exponents of sand play than the Shark. Here he has thrilled the crowd on his way to victory in the 1986 British Open.

Following pages: Legends on the march. Norman is in exalted company alongside Lee Trevino, Jack Nicklaus and Tom Watson, hitting off in a practice round before the 1987 British Open.

Above: The most recognisable figure on the world golf circuit stands alone as golf fairway links with broad ocean.

that we have been able to keep tabs on Greg's progress in world golf. On the all-conquering 1989 Ashes tour of England we were playing Gloucestershire in Bristol in a three-day game. I thought I had planned everything to perfection so as to be batting on the Sunday, which would enable us to watch the final round of the British Open. Well, the best-laid plans went horribly wrong and we were bowled out before tea, just as the golf was getting exciting. Greg was in the clubhouse, having shot the lights out in his final round to be right there in contention, and Wayne Grady was still out on the course with the leaders. So, amidst much grumbling from our boys, we had to go out and field, seemingly missing the pulsating finale to the championship.

But Geoff Lawson opened the bowling and started brilliantly. Wickets tumbled. At every break in play the 12th man would run onto the field with an update on the golf. 'Henry' Lawson continued to bowl well, taking wickets at regular intervals and the golf got more and more interesting—except we weren't watching!

During the last session Geoff grabbed six or seven wickets and we won, having knocked Gloucestershire over inside the session. It was the only time I had seen, at the fall of the last wicket, every player race off the ground before the batsmen—and without giving Geoff a much-deserved clap for his efforts. The simple reason: the golf was on!

Above: Back to business and yet another trophy capture.

We crowded around the television to witness an incredible situation. There was a three-way play-off involving Greg Norman, Wayne Grady and Mark Calcavecchia. We were confident of an Aussie victory. Famous last words! Calcavecchia won and Greg was robbed again!

I've been fortunate to have been to the US Masters on two occasions. Without doubt, it is one of the great sporting events. It is a tournament that Greg generally plays extremely well, although he probably has mixed feelings towards Augusta because of the heartache he has experienced there over the years.

My first visit to Augusta was in 1992, a couple of years after the famous (or infamous) Larry Mize chip-in at the 11th hole during the play-off for the Masters to once again deny Greg the coveted Green Jacket. That part of the course is known as Amen Corner and is spectacular. The shot Mize played that day has haunted me for years. After play had finished on the second day I took a stroll down to the 11th hole and stood behind the roped-off area, pondering that shot. Curiosity got the better of me and I ducked under the rope and went to the very spot Larry Mize had chipped from. It is impossible to imagine getting the ball within 10 feet, let alone sinking it! I don't think it could be done again!

I got to know Greg a lot better on my second visit to the Masters when Pat Welsh, a close friend of both Greg's and mine, organised for me, together with Dean Jones and Jim Tait, to go down to Florida to play some golf at Greg's course, The Medallist, and catch up with the Shark. We had a great time (the course was real tough, and my golf ordinary) and then went back to Greg's house on Jupiter Island for a few beers and a barbeque. We asked him the usual questions about how he coped with the pressures and the near-misses at the 'big ones'. We talked about cricket, football, politics, even US tax laws (Jim Tait's area of expertise).

Greg was right up to speed on everything, even giving 'Jonesy' a hard time over a much-publicised spat with Bob Simpson. To cap the night off (while drinking some Grange Hermitage), Greg decided that it would be a good idea to ring Nick Price, a great friend of his and who lived just down the road. Nick dragged himself out of bed, joined the party, and we all lounged around having a great old time. Greg and Nick, at the time arguably the two best golfers in the world, ended up bagging each other's putting stroke. I'm just glad they didn't decide to dissect my game!

The whole night was a ripper and I found Greg to be a brilliant bloke, a dinkum Aussie who genuinely loves Australia and loved having some Aussies over for a beer and a chat.

He is, without doubt, one of Australia's greatest ambassadors and a real hero of mine.

Below: Putting is a serious business. Norman is a study of concentration at the 1996 US Open at Oakland Hills. Opposite: Time to contemplate.

It was the only time I had seen, at the fall of the last wicket, every player race off the ground before the batsmen ... The simple reason: the golf was on!

IN THE FAST LANE

by Renton Laidlaw

Edinburgh-born Renton Laidlaw is the Marco Polo of golf trekking. Constantly on tour, he once covered 48 tournaments in 52 weeks. He is the author of nine books and a highly popular television commentator in his colourful Scottish brogue. He salutes Greg Norman as golf's Man of Action.

Greg Norman, world traveller and golfer extraordinaire, lives his life the way he drives his cars—fast, when he gets the chance. He is golf's action man whose daily timetable seldom includes an afternoon off and whose work rate is unmatched by almost any other golfer, with the exception over the years of workaholic Gary Player.

The busier the Shark is the more he seems to like it, whether playing with complete commitment in a tournament or enjoying just as much an involvement in those often delicate boardroom negotiations that have helped him build up an impressive and constantly expanding business empire.

Greg Norman is 'hands on'—a winner both on and off the course, driven constantly by the desire to be the best. Of course he is golf's biggest all-time prize-winner in terms of dollars—he was first to surpass $US10 million on the US Tour and worldwide has won half as much again—but these days his big money is made from his multifarious businesses which range from designing courses, growing special types of grass, and helping design his own range of quality clothing, to giving his name to his own-recipe (or is it wife Laura's?) pasta sauce.

Golf, and the way he plays it, has enabled him to succeed in ventures far removed from the sport. Today, many who buy Greg Norman products are not golfers and do not even know he plays

Page 105: Golf's 'man of action' astride a Harley Davidson during a Harley feature in Singapore, 1996.

Opposite: Greg Norman's marketing value was recognised from his early arrival on the American stage, to the extent of this workable scene high in the rockies in Colorado. Immaculate in a dinner suit, this wasn't a modelling assignment. That's a golf ball in his hand in the manufacturer's ambitious promotion of sales.

Above: The golf bag serves the purpose as Norman and his caddie, Steve Williams, take a break at the 1988 Australian Open at Royal Sydney.

Opposite: It's the Australian Masters at Huntingdale 1991, familiar and favoured territory for the Shark who has won the prestigious event five times.

the game. The Florida-based 44-year-old Queenslander who has always said that one day, when he is ready to retire, he will return to his Australian roots, is more than a golfing icon; he is the personification of what can be achieved if, assuming you have the talent in the first place, you are willing to work hard to exploit it to the full.

The game would have been the loser had the young Norman actually gone on to a career in the Royal Australian Air Force. He knew he would love flying supersonic jets and for a time wanted nothing else but, happily, he decided he could fly even higher and achieve super status much faster at ground level! How right he was when he realised that his golf clubs would be far more effective than a jet-plane joystick in satisfying his desire to make himself a fortune and, more importantly, his zest for life.

When you have made as much money these days as Norman has and spent it wisely, you have little need to use the prize-money dollar as an incentive. Money has long since ceased to be his motivation. In golfing terms, he still has unfulfilled goals and still dreams of adding to his two major victories in the Open Championship. Before he finally calls it a day it would be nice, for instance, for Greg to win an American major and, in particular, a Masters Green Jacket.

Golf has been good for Greg Norman but it has also served up its fair share of disappointments. Of course, sometimes those setbacks have been of his own making; a slack shot played under pressure, for instance, but often, especially in the case of Bob Tway, who holed a bunker shot to beat him in the 1986 US PGA Championship or Larry Mize who, one year later, holed an outrageous downhill 160-foot pitch to beat him at Augusta, he has been a victim of cruel circumstances.

It is generally accepted that a golfer's international success is measured by the number of grand slam titles won. Norman's tally of two, compared with close friend Jack Nicklaus's 18, seems a completely inadequate expression of his playing ability and competitive qualities since turning professional in 1976, or of the impact he has had on the game.

One record Norman—ironically one of the game's toughest competitors—would rather not be associated with is the dubious one of lost major titles in every possible way: over 18 holes to Fuzzy Zoeller in the 1984 US Open, in sudden death to Mize at Augusta and to Paul Azinger in the 1993 US PGA Championship, and over four holes of stroke-play to Mark Calcavecchia in the Open at Troon in 1989. His majors record shows he has been in the top five 17 times and won twice, compared with contemporary Nick Faldo's 18 top-five finishes and six wins.

Like almost every great sporting hero, Norman is a complex character capable of acts of tremendous generosity, more often than not, carried out quietly, well away from the television

Above: The interviewers are rarely far away from the Shark during a tournament rampage.

Opposite, top: Greg Norman fits into a business suit as easily as his golf attire. Here the Shark unfurls design plans for one of his many course construction contracts. Golf course construction is a major part of his burgeoning business interests.

Opposite, bottom: Norman is in his element in the 1993 British Open fray at Royal St George's.

cameras. A dedicated family man, he has a far softer heart than he would care to have you know. The public image that must be maintained is that of a no-nonsense, tight-lipped golfing 'killer' with clear blue eyes that can burn ferociously. This may mean that at times when he is completely cocooned in 'the zone' he can be single-mindedly awkward. But anyone who has been on the short end of Greg's more temperamental self would do well to remember that all great players need to have fire in their bellies to achieve what they do on the course. Without an occasional mean streak, would Nicklaus have achieved all he did? Or Player, or Faldo, or Seve Ballesteros, or even the ambassadorial figure of Peter Thomson who perhaps did not have to endure the constant media attention Norman has had to deal with over the years?

All great sportsmen living their lives in a goldfish-bowl environment with their every action or comment analysed—not always sympathetically—must be self-centred at times. To maintain their occasional god-like status in the game they often feel they have to adopt a somewhat selfish and maybe even unreasonable attitude in order to emphasise that they are in control. Greg is no different, but to judge him on those few, but too often recalled incidents when, on reflection, he may have regretted his own behaviour, would be grossly unfair. No modern-day golfer, other than Nick Faldo, who has often been his own worst enemy, has been the victim of a hostile press more than Norman, but he never ignores his obligations in this respect.

He has been a generous winner more than 70 times but, more impressively, Norman is a far more gracious loser than many of his contemporaries. One of his most traumatic defeats was that inflicted by Faldo in the 1996 Masters when he went into the final round six in front and lost to the British player by five—a defeat that might well have inflicted so much psychological damage as to finish any other player's career. It did not finish Norman. Three years later he was up there again at Augusta, tied for the lead with five to play before losing to Jose Maria Olazabal who charged home in 31. Even Olazabal felt for Norman that week, but not until he had all but won the Green Jacket.

Significantly, Olazabal deliberately waited for Norman to join him for that final 100-yard walk up the hill to the green below the Augusta clubhouse. It was a gesture from one friend to another, a token of the great respect Olazabal, who himself fought back after a near career-threatening injury, has always had for the man who had refused to abandon his competitive career even after requiring extensive shoulder surgery.

Norman had the chance to give up a year ago but refused to do so because playing golf competitively is so important to him, as long as he feels he has the chance to win. The buzz he gets from

playing himself into contention—these days often against players much younger—is addictive, which is good news for those who enjoy watching a golfing cavalier who plays the game with a showmanlike panache missing in many others.

Golf may have been the vehicle enabling Greg Norman to amass a huge fortune but there is no doubt that the blond-haired Australian with the hard-man good looks of Clint Eastwood has played an important role in popularising the game internationally. How many have been drawn to golf in the past 25 years simply by watching him and by being impressed at the exciting way he plays?

His golf game is very different from the one most of us play and enjoy, but it is the game of a man who has done it his way and done it well. If ever he were to win the Masters at Augusta the world of golf would see it as a well-deserved reward for one who has played the game with total integrity throughout his career. Never forget (while the money rolls in these days to the Shark's bank account) that what he has achieved—and still is achieving in a game built on the firm foundation of honesty and fair play—has been the result of hard graft then and now. His sponsors over the years have always known that with Greg Norman they were dealing with an honest broker who has always given them and his army of fans value for money. Long may he want to play and long may we enjoy his own brand of quality golf.

Below: In a burst of flying sand, Norman extricates from danger from this bunker in the 1990 Australian Open at the Australian Golf Club.
Opposite: The Shark emerges from the shadows at St. Andrews during play at the Dunhill Cup in Scotland.

He knew he would love flying supersonic jets and for a time wanted nothing else but, happily, he decided he could fly even higher and achieve super status much faster at ground level.

How right he was ...

STATISTICS

1976

TOURNAMENT VICTORIES: One
- West Lakes Classic, The Grange Golf Club (G.C.), 64–67–66–74–271; won by five strokes.

WORLD STROKE AVERAGE—Outside top 50 placings. First, Jack Nicklaus (70.5).
WORLD MONEY LIST PLACING—Outside top 200 placings. Leader, Jack Nicklaus ($316,086)*.

1977

TOURNAMENT VICTORIES: Two
- Martini International Tournament, Blairgowrie G.C., 70–71–70–66–277; won by three.
- Kuzuha Kokusai, Kuzuha Public G.C., 69–66–135; won by two.

THE MAJORS
- Missed 54-hole cut, British Open, Turnberry G.C., 78–72–74–224. Tom Watson (268).

WORLD STROKE AVERAGE—Tied equal 50th, 71.89. First, Tom Watson (70.24).
WORLD MONEY LIST PLACING—95th, $51,225. Leader, Tom Watson ($358,034).

1978

TOURNAMENT VICTORIES: Four
- Caltex Festival of Sydney Open, The Lakes G.C., 73–69–72–64–278; won by three.
- Traralgon Loy Yang Classic, Traralgon G.C., 71–70–69–67–277; won by one.
- Gilbey's South Sea Classic, Pacific Harbour G.C. (Fiji), 73–71–73–71–288; won sudden-death play-off.
- New South Wales Open, Manly G.C., 64–72–69–70–275; won by three.

THE MAJORS
- Tied equal 29th, British Open, St. Andrews G.C., 72–73–74–72–291: Jack Nicklaus (281).

WORLD STROKE AVERAGE—Tied equal 46th, 71.79. First, Lee Trevino (70.24).
WORLD MONEY LIST PLACING—75th, $69,754. Leader, Tom Watson ($384,388).
WORLD RANKING—Outside top 25. First, Tom Watson (450.5).

1979

TOURNAMENT VICTORIES: Three
- Traralgon Loy Yang Classic, Traralgon G.C., 69–65–71–72–277; won by three.
- Cathay Pacific Hong Kong Open, Royal Hong Kong G.C., 70–66–69–68–273; won by three.
- Martini International, Wentworth G.C., 75–67–72–74–288; won by one.

THE MAJORS

- Tied equal 48th, US Open, Inverness G.C., 76–74–74–78–302; Hale Irwin (284).
- Tied equal 10th, British Open, Royal Lytham & St. Annes G.C., 73–71–72–76–292; Severiano Ballesteros (283).

WORLD STROKE AVERAGE—Outside top 50 placings. First, Tom Watson (70.61).

WORLD MONEY LIST PLACING—59th, $97,968. Leader, Tom Watson ($506,912).

WORLD RANKING—21st (120.5 points). First, Tom Watson (515).

1980

TOURNAMENT VICTORIES: Four

- French Open, Golf de Saint-Cloud, 67–66–68–67–268; won by 10.
- Scandinavian Enterprises Open, Vasatorps G.C., 76–66–70–64–276; won by three.
- Suntory World Match Play Championship, Wentworth G.C. (West).
- Dunhill Australian Open, The Lakes G.C., 71–70–73–70–284; won by one.

THE MAJORS

- Missed 54-hole cut, British Open, Muirfield Golf Links, 74–74–76–224: Tom Watson (271).

WORLD STROKE AVERAGE—Tied equal 26th, 71.33. First, Lee Trevino (69.75).

WORLD MONEY LIST PLACING—11th, $242,874. Leader, Tom Watson ($651,921).

CAREER MONEY LIST PLACING—Outside top 50 placings. Leader, Jack Nicklaus ($4,283,865).

WORLD RANKING—13th (173 points). First, Tom Watson (541.5).

1981

TOURNAMENT VICTORIES: Three

- Martini International, Wentworth G.C., 71–72–72–72–287; won by one.
- Dunlop Masters, Woburn Golf and Country Club (G.&C.C.), 72–68–66–67–273; won by four.
- Australian Masters, Huntingdale G.C., 67–77–71–74–289; won by seven.

THE MAJORS

- Fourth, US Masters, Augusta National G.C., 69–70–72–72–283; Tom Watson (280).
- Tied equal 23rd, US Open, Merion G.C., 71–67–73–76–287; David Graham (273).
- Tied equal 31st, British Open, Royal St. George's, 72–75–72–72–291; Bill Rogers (276).
- Tied equal fourth, US PGA, Atlanta Athletic Club, 73–67–68–71–279; Larry Nelson (273).

WORLD STROKE AVERAGE—Tied equal 20th, 71.18. First, Tom Kite (69.86).

WORLD MONEY LIST PLACING—21st, $218,249. Leader, Johnny Miller ($704,204).

CAREER MONEY LIST PLACING—Outside top 50 placings. Leader, Jack Nicklaus ($4,594,516).

WORLD RANKING—13th (202 points). First, Tom Watson (435.5).

1982

TOURNAMENT VICTORIES: Three

- Dunlop Masters, St. Pierre G.&C.C., 68–69–65–65–267; won by eight.
- State Express Classic, The Belfry (Brabazon), 70–70–70–69–279; won by one.
- Benson & Hedges International Open, Fulford, 69–74–69–71–283; won by one.

THE MAJORS

- Tied equal 36th, US Masters, Augusta National G.C., 73–75–73–79–300: Craig Stadler (284).
- Tied equal 27th, British Open, Royal Troon, 73–75–76–72–296: Tom Watson (284).
- Tied equal fifth, US PGA, Southern Hills Country Club (C.C.), 66–69–70–72–277: Raymond Floyd (272).

WORLD STROKE AVERAGE—44th, 71.46. First, Calvin Peete (70.28).

WORLD MONEY LIST PLACING—23rd, $226,059. Leader, Ray Floyd ($738,669).

CAREER MONEY LIST PLACING—Outside top 50 placings.

WORLD RANKING—12th (188 pts). First, Tom Watson (366).

1983

TOUNAMENT VICTORIES: Seven

- Kapalua International, Kapalua Bay G.C., 67–69–65–67–268: won by six.
- Suntory World Match Play, Wentworth G.C. (West).
- Open de Cannes-Mougins, Cannes-Mougins C.C., 69–74–72–72–287; won by two.
- Australian Masters, Huntingdale G.C., 74–67–78–66–285; won by four.
- Stefan Queensland Open, Royal Queensland G.C., 67–68–70–72–277; won by one.
- National Panasonic New South Wales Open, Concord G.C., 75–68–67–68–278; won sudden-death play-off.
- Cathay Pacific Hong Kong Open, Royal Hong Kong G.C., 68–66–134; won by three.

THE MAJORS

- Tied equal 30th, US Masters, Augusta National G.C., 71–74–70–79–294: Severiano Ballesteros (280).
- Tied equal 50th, US Open, Oakmont C.C., 74–75–81–72–302: Larry Nelson (280).
- Tied equal 19th, British Open, Royal Birkdale G.C., 75–71–70–67–283: Tom Watson (275).
- Tied equal 42nd, US PGA, Riviera C.C., 72–72–70–75–289: Hal Sutton (274).

WORLD STROKE AVERAGE—24th, 71.15. First, Nick Faldo (70.15).

WORLD MONEY LIST PLACING—11th, $366,819. Leader, Severiano Ballesteros ($686,088).

CAREER MONEY LIST PLACING—44th, $1,290,308. Leader, Jack Nicklaus ($5,230,924).

WORLD RANKING—Fourth, (236 points). First, Severiano Ballesteros (328.5).

1984

TOURNAMENT VICTORIES: Five

- Kemper Open, Congressional C.C., 68–68–71–73–280; won by five.
- Canadian Open, Glen Abbey G.C., 73–68–70–67–278; won by two.
- Victorian Open, Metropolitan G.C., 70–71–68–72–281; won by two.
- Australian Masters, Huntingdale G.C., 74–71–70–70–285; won by three.
- Toshiba Australian PGA, Monash C.C., 66–71–71–69–277; won by eight.

THE MAJORS

- Tied equal 25th, US Masters, Augusta National G.C., 75–71–73–69–288; Ben Crenshaw (277).
- Second, US Open, Winged Foot G.C., 70–68–69–69–276; lost 18–hole play-off to Fuzzy Zoeller (75–67).
- Tied equal 39th, US PGA, Shoal Creek G.C., 75–72–73–71–291; Lee Trevino (273).

WORLD STROKE AVERAGE—Tied equal 10th, 70.85. First, Sandy Lyle (70.00).

WORLD MONEY LIST PLACING—Third, $533,405. Leader, Severiano Ballesteros ($668,047).

CAREER MONEY LIST PLACING—27th, $1,823,713. Leader, Jack Nicklaus ($5,521,620).

WORLD RANKING—Third (281.5 points). First, Severiano Ballesteros (368.5).

1985

TOURNAMENT VICTORIES: Two, plus Dunhill Cup, St. Andrews (teams)—refer to 1986.

- Toshiba Australian PGA, Castle Hill G.C., 70–68–66–69–273; won by eight.
- National Panasonic Australian Open, Royal Melbourne G.C., 67–71–74–212; won by two.

THE MAJORS

- Tied equal 47th, US Masters, Augusta National G.C., 73–72–75–78–298; Bernhard Langer (282).
- Tied equal 15th, US Open, Oakland Hills C.C., 72–71–71–72–286; Andy North (279).
- Tied equal 16th, British Open, Royal St. George's G.C., 71–72–71–73–287; Sandy Lyle (282).
- Missed 36-hole cut, US PGA, Cherry Hills C.C., 75–73–148; Hubert Green (278).

WORLD STROKE AVERAGE—22nd, 70.95. First, Severiano Ballesteros (70.22).

WORLD MONEY LIST PLACING—15th, $392,720. Leader, Bernhard Langer ($860,262).

CAREER MONEY LIST PLACING—25th, $2,216,433. Leader, Jack Nicklaus ($5,688,776).

WORLD RANKING—Third, (263 points). First, Severiano Ballesteros (362.5).

1986

TOURNAMENT VICTORIES: Nine, plus Dunhill Cup teams event.

- Las Vegas Invitational, Las Vegas C.C., Desert Inn C.C., Spanish Trail G.&C.C., 73–63–68–64–65–333; won by seven.
- Kemper Open, Congressional C.C., 72–69–70–66–277; won sudden-death play-off.
- British Open, Turnberry G.C., 74–63–74–69–280; won by five.
- Panasonic European Open, Sunningdale G.C. (Old), 67–67–69–66–269; won sudden-death play-off.
- Dunhill Cup, St. Andrews G.C., four wins, 67–67–70–73–277.
- Suntory World Match Play, Wentworth G.C. (West).
- Stefan Queensland Open, Coolangatta–Tweed Heads G.C., 67–70–70–70–277; won by six.
- National Panasonic New South Wales Open, Concord G.C., 65–70–67–73–275; won by five.
- West End Jubilee South Australia Open, Kooyonga G.C., 75–68–75–65–283; won by three.
- National Panasonic Western Australian Open, Lake Karrinyup C.C., 72–70–66–68–276; won by one.

THE MAJORS

- Tied equal second, US Masters, Augusta National G.C., 70–72–68–70–280; Jack Nicklaus (279).
- Tied equal 12th, US Open, Shinnecock Hills G.C., 71–68–71–75–285; Raymond Floyd (279).
- First, British Open, Turnberry G.C., 74–63–74–69–280; won by five.
- Second, US PGA, Inverness G.C, 65–68–69–76–278; Bob Tway (276).

WORLD STROKE AVERAGE—Fourth, 70.01. First, Severiano Ballesteros, (69.68)

WORLD MONEY LIST PLACING—First, $1,146,584.

CAREER MONEY LIST PLACING—13th, $3,363,017. Leader, Jack Nicklaus ($5,938,309).

WORLD RANKING—First (1,507 points).

1987

TOURNAMENT VICTORIES: Two

- Australian Masters, Huntingdale G.C., 68–67–68–70–273; won by nine.
- National Panasonic Australian Open, Royal Melbourne G.C., 70–66–66–71–273; won by 10.

THE MAJORS

- Tied equal second, US Masters, Augusta National G.C., 73–74–66–72–285; lost play-off to Larry Mize.
- Tied equal 51st, US Open, Olympic Club (Lakeside), 72–69–74–77–292; Scott Simpson (277).
- Tied equal 35th, British Open, Muirfield, 71–71–74–75–291; Nick Faldo (279).
- Seventieth, US PGA, PGA National G.C. (Champions), 73–78–79–79–309; Larry Nelson (287).

WORLD MONEY LIST PLACING—Fifth, $715,838. Leader, Ian Woosnam ($1,793,268).

CAREER MONEY LIST PLACING—Ninth, $4,066,730. Leader, Jack Nicklaus ($6,028,010).

WORLD RANKING—First (1,231 points).

1988

TOURNAMENT VICTORIES: Six

- MCI Heritage Classic, Harbour Town Golf Links, 65–69–71–66–271; won by one.
- Lancia Italian Open, Monticello G.C., 69–68–63–70–270; won by one.
- Daikyo Palm Meadows Cup, Palm Meadows G.C., 69–66–67–70–272; won by one.
- ESP Open, Royal Canberra G.C., 62–70–69–68–269; won by seven.
- Australian Tournament Players' Championship, Riverside Oaks PGA National, 67–67–68–68–270; won by eight.
- Panasonic New South Wales Open, Concord G.C., 66–69–69–73–277; won by one.

THE MAJORS

- Tied equal fifth, US Masters, Augusta National G.C., 77–73–71–64–285; Sandy Lyle (281).
- Withdrew; US Open, The Country Club; Curtis Strange (278).
- Did not compete, British Open, Royal Lytham & St. Annes G.C.; Severiano Ballesteros (273).
- Tied equal ninth, US PGA, Oak Tree G.C., 68–71–72–71–282; Jeff Sluman (272).

WORLD MONEY LIST PLACING—Ninth, $957,497. Leader, Severiano Ballesteros ($1,261,275).
CAREER MONEY LIST PLACING—Fourth, $5,024,227. Leader, Jack Nicklaus ($6,078,922).
WORLD RANKING—Second (1,365 points). First, Severiano Ballesteros (1,458).

1989

TOURNAMENT VICTORIES: Five
- The International, Castle Pines G.C., 13 points; won by two points.
- Greater Milwaukee Open, Tuckaway C.C., 64–69–66–70–269; won by three.
- Australian Masters, Huntingdale G.C., 69–69–74–68–280; won by five.
- Australian Tournament Players' Championship, Riverside Oaks PGA National, 70–70–69–67–276; won by two.
- Cunichi Crowns, Nagoya G.C. (Wago), 65–68–71–68–272; won by three.

THE MAJORS
- Tied equal third, US Masters, Augusta National G.C., 74–75–68–67–284; Nick Faldo (283).
- Tied equal 33rd, US Open, Oak Hill C.C., 72–68–73–76–289; Curtis Strange (278).
- Tied equal second, British Open, Royal Troon G.C., 69–70–72–64–275; lost play-off to Mark Calcavecchia.
- Tied equal 12th, US PGA, Kemper Lakes G.C., 74–71–67–70–282; Payne Stewart (276).
WORLD MONEY LIST PLACING—Third $1,351,761. Leader, David Frost ($1,650,230).
CAREER MONEY LIST PLACING—Second, $6,375,988. Leader, Severiano Ballesteros ($6,573,553).
WORLD RANKING—First (1,385 points).

1990

TOURNAMENT VICTORIES: Three
- Australian Masters, Huntingdale G.C., 68–67–70–68–273; won by two.
- Doral Ryder Open, Doral Resort & C.C., 68–73–70–62–273; won sudden-death play-off.
- Memorial Tournament, Muirfield Village G.C., 73–74–69–216; won by one.

THE MAJORS
- Missed 36-hole cut, US Masters, Augusta National G.C.; Nick Faldo (278).
- Tied equal fifth, US Open, Medinah C.C., 72–73–69–69–283; Hale Irwin (280).
- Tied equal sixth, British Open, St. Andrews G.C. (Old), 66–66–76–69–277; Nick Faldo (270).
- Tied equal 19th, US PGA, Shoal Creek C.C., 77–69–76–73–295; Wayne Grady (282).
WORLD MONEY LIST PLACING—Third, $1,457,378. Leader Jose Maria Olazabal ($1,633,640).
CAREER MONEY LIST PLACING—First, $8,015,366.
WORLD RANKING—First (1,402 points).

1991

TOURNAMENT VICTORIES: nil

THE MAJORS
- Missed 36-hole cut, US Masters, Augusta National G.C., 78–69–147; Ian Woosnam (277).
- Withdrew, US Open, Hazeltine National G.C., 78, wd; Payne Stewart (282).
- Tied equal ninth, British Open, Royal Birkdale G.C., 74–68–71–66–279; Ian Baker-Finch (272).
- Tied equal 32nd, US PGA, Crooked Stick Club, 70–74–72–73–289; John Daly (276).
WORLD MONEY LIST PLACING—29th, $753,092. Leader, Bernhard Langer ($2,186,700).
CAREER MONEY LIST PLACING—First, $8,768,458.
WORLD RANKING—Fifth (957 points). First, Ian Woosnam (1,249).

1992

TOURNAMENT VICTORIES: One
- Canadian Open, Glen Abbey G.C., 73–66–71–70–280; won sudden-death play-off.

THE MAJORS

- Tied equal sixth, US Masters, Augusta National G.C., 70–70–73–68–281; Fred Couples (275).
- Did not compete, US Open, Pebble Beach Golf Links; Tom Kite (285).
- Eighteenth, British Open, Muirfield, 71–72–70–68–281; Nick Faldo (272).
- Tied equal 15th, US PGA, Bellerive C.C., 71–74–71–70–286; Nick Price (278).

WORLD MONEY LIST PLACING—10th, $1,240,771. Leader, Nick Faldo ($2,748,248).

CAREER MONEY LIST PLACING—First, $10,009,229.

WORLD RANKING—Fifth (887 points). First, Nick Faldo (1,648 points).

1993

TOURNAMENT VICTORIES: Two

- Doral Ryder Open, Doral Resort & C.C. (Blue Monster), 65–68–62–70–265; won by four.
- British Open, Royal St. George's G.C., 66–68–69–64–267; won by two.

THE MAJORS

- Tied equal 31st, US Masters, Augusta National G.C., 74–68–71–77–290; Bernhard Langer (277).
- Missed 36-hole cut, US Open, Baltusrol G.C., 73–74–147; Lee Janzen (272).
- First, British Open, Royal St. George's G.C., 66–68–69–64–267; won by two.

WORLD MONEY LIST PLACING—Not available (earnings at September 7, $1,363,728).

CAREER MONEY LIST PLACING—First, $11,372,957.

WORLD RANKING—(as at September 7) second (19.36 points); First, Nick Faldo (22.28 points).

1994

TOURNAMENT VICTORIES: Three

- The Players' Championship, Sawgrass, 63–67–67–67–264; won by four.
- PGA Grand Slam of Golf, Kauai, 70–66–136; won by three.
- Johnnie Walker Asia Classic, Blue Canyon C.C., 75–70–64–68–277; won by one.

THE MAJORS

- Tied equal 18th, US Masters, Augusta National G.C., 70–70–75–77–292; Jose-Maria Olazabal (279).
- Tied equal sixth, US Open, Oakmont C.C., 71–71–69–72–283; Ernie Els (279) play-off.
- Tied equal 11th, British Open, Turnberry G.C., 71–67–69–69–276; Nick Price (269).
- Tied equal fourth, US PGA,, Southern Hills C.C., 71–69–67–70–277; Nick Price (269).

WORLD MONEY LIST PLACING—Fifth, $2,117,307. Leader, Ernie Els ($2,862,854).

CAREER MONEY LIST PLACING—First, $14,411,816.

WORLD RANKING—Second (20.57 points). First, Nick Price (21.19).

1995

TOURNAMENT VICTORIES: Five

- Memorial Tournament, Muirfield Village G.C., 66–70–67–66–269; won by four.
- Greater Hartford Open, River Highlands, Connecticut, 67–64–65–71–267; won by two.
- World Series of Golf, Firestone C.C., Akron, 66–70–67–66–269; won sudden-death play-off.
- Heineken Australian Open, Kingston Heath G.C., 72–69–69–68–278; won by two.
- Fred Meyer Challenge, West Linn, Oregon, Norman–Brad Faxon, 65–64–129; won play-off.

THE MAJORS

- Tied equal third, US Masters, Augusta National G.C., 73–68–68–68–277; Ben Crenshaw (274).
- Second, US Open, Shinnecock Hills, 68–67–74–73–282; Corey Pavin (280).
- Tied equal 15th, British Open, St. Andrews G.C., 71–74–72–70–287; John Daly (282).
- Tied equal 20th, US PGA, Riviera C.C., 66–69–70–72–277; Steve Elkington (267).

WORLD MONEY LIST PLACING—Fourth, $2,001,285. Leader, Corey Pavin ($2,746,340).

CAREER MONEY LIST PLACING—First, $16,413,101.

WORLD RANKING—First, (21.97 points).

1996

TOURNAMENT VICTORIES: Five

- South Australian Open, Kooyonga G.C., 74–72–69–69–284; won by one.
- Holden Australian Open, The Australian G.C., 67–73–71–69–280; won by eight.
- Doral-Ryder Open, Doral Resort C.C., 67–69–67–66–269; won by two.
- Fred Meyer Challenge, West Linn, 63–61–124; won by one.
- Anderson Consulting World Championships, Grayhawk, Scottsdale. (def. Hoch 1 up in final).

THE MAJORS

- Second, US Masters, Augusta National G.C., 63–69–71–78–281; Nick Faldo (276).
- Tied equal 10th, US Open, Oakland Hills G.C., 73–66–74–70–283; Steve Jones (278).
- Tied equal seventh, British Open, Royal Lytham & St. Annes G.C., 71–68–71–67–277; Tom Lehman (271).
- Tied equal 17th, US PGA, Valhalla G.C., 68–72–69–73–282; Mark Brooks (277, play-off).

WORLD MONEY LIST PLACING—Third, $2,258,678. Leader, Colin Montgomerie ($3,071,442).

CAREER MONEY LIST PLACING—First, $18,671,779.

WORLD RANKING—First (10.78 points).

1997

TOURNAMENT VICTORIES: Three

- St. Jude Classic, Southwind G.C., 68–65–69–66–268; won by one.
- World Series of Golf, Firestone C.C., 68–68–70–67–273; won by four.
- Fred Meyer Challenge, Oregon G.C., Norman–Brad Faxon, 60–63–123; won by three.

THE MAJORS

- Missed 36-hole cut, US Masters, Augusta National G.C., 77–74–151; Tiger Woods (270).
- Missed 36-hole cut, US Open, Congressional, 75–79–154; Ernie Els (276).
- Tied 36th, British Open, Royal Troon G.C., 69–73–70–75–287; Justin Leonard (272).
- Tied 13th, US PGA, Winged Foot G.C., 68–71–74–71–284; Davis Love III (269).

WORLD MONEY LIST PLACING—Eighth, $1,949,508. Leader, Tiger Woods ($2,082,381).

CAREER MONEY LIST PLACING—First, $20,621,287.

WORLD RANKING—First (11.49 points).

1998

TOURNAMENT VICTORIES: Two

- Greg Norman Holden International, The Australian G.C., 68–73–64–67–272; won by two.
- Franklin Templeton Shark Shootout, Sherwood C.C.; won play-off.

THE MAJORS

Out of action for seven months because of shoulder surgery, missing all four majors.

WORLD MONEY LIST PLACING—148th, $354,479.

CAREER MONEY LIST PLACING—First, $20,975,766.

WORLD RANKING—18th (5.65 points).

Note: Prizemoney winnings are in U.S. dollars.